Day Wa
Peak District

20 classic circular routes

VERTEBRATE PUBLISHING

Design and production by Vertebrate Publishing, Sheffield
www.v-publishing.co.uk

Day Walks in the PeakDistrict

20 classic circular routes

Written by
Norman Taylor & Barry Pope

Day Walks in the **PeakDistrict**

20 classic circular routes

VG Copyright © 2012 **Vertebrate Graphics Ltd** and **Norman Taylor & Barry Pope**.

VP First published in 2005 by **Vertebrate Publishing**.
This second edition first published in 2012 by **Vertebrate Publishing**.

ISBN 978-1-906148-49-2

Cover photo: Lower Wolfscote Dale (route 16). Photo: John Coefield.
Back cover photo: Ladybower Reservoir from Whinstone Lee Tor (route 3).
Photo: Jon Barton

Photography as credited.

All maps reproduced by permission of Ordnance Survey on behalf
of The Controller of Her Majesty's Stationery Office.
© Crown Copyright. 100025218

Design and production by Nathan Ryder – www.**v-graphics**.co.uk

MIX
Paper from
responsible sources
FSC® C010256
www.fsc.org

Printed in China.

Contents

WHITE EDGE MOOR PHOTO: JOHN COEFIELD

Introduction

The walks described in this guide all fall within the Peak District National Park. They are evenly spread throughout the area, and reflect the great variety of landscape, flora, fauna and human settlement within the national park boundary.

The geology of the Peak has resulted in the formation of two distinct types of landscape, one defined as the Dark Peak, the other the White Peak. The moors and craggy edges in the north and to the east and west of the central area were shaped by underlying layers of sandstone of a hard, gritty consistency. This rock, known as millstone grit because it was used to make high quality millstones, becomes dark on exposure to the elements. This area is the Dark Peak.

Beneath the sandstone is a thick layer of carboniferous limestone. Where the sandstones have disappeared through erosion in the central and southern Peak, this grey-white rock has shaped the landscape. It is an area of rolling upland with occasional outcrops and deep, crag-lined limestone gorges, the part of the Peak District known as the White Peak.

Each year millions of people are drawn to the Peak District to see the sights, to climb its crags, to ride bikes along its bridleways and byways, and to explore the area on foot. If you come into the last category, we hope this guide helps you sample and enjoy the diversity of this beautiful countryside.

So, take your pick, explore, enjoy, tell your friends.

Norman Taylor & Barry Pope

Acknowledgements

The authors would like to thank the following people for their help in various ways:

Gess Boothby and Wendy Brown, Ian (Hovis) and Jacqui Brown for sterling work checking out route descriptions and highlighting any need for amendment; Dave Jepson for constructive suggestions for walks; Dave Pandya, Paul Dolling and Sarah Deakin, all of Foothills, for their willingness to be guinea pigs in testing some of the routes; Maureen Po for acting as courier; Matt and Sam Taylor for their technical assistance with the PC; and Norman's wife, Sue, for her encouragement and support.

About the walks

All the walks are 'day' walks in the sense that they take 4 to 8 hours at an unhurried pace. They fall into three broad categories of terrain: walks on the high moors; walks on low lying hills, tors and edges; walks in limestone country.

The **summary** and **route description** for each walk should be studied carefully before setting out on a walk. Together they describe the terrain involved, the amount of ascent and the level of navigation skills required.

Walk times

The times given are reasonably generous while giving a guideline for planning purposes. If you're unsure how fast or slow you walk, start off with one of the shorter routes and progress to the longer ones once you're sure.

Navigation

As a rule, the description and map should be enough to get around safely and accurately, but it's always worth carrying a back-up copy of the relevant OS or Harvey Map, in case you inadvertently travel off the page, or need to change your route for any reason.

Ordnance Survey Explorer® OL1 (1:25,000) The Dark Peak
Ordnance Survey Explorer® OL24 (1:25,000) The White Peak
Harvey British Mountain Map (1:40,000) Dark Peak
Harvey Dark Peak Superwalker Map (1:25,000) Dark Peak

GPS

A GPS can be a useful navigational aid and is well worth carrying. But always carry spare batteries – they do tend to run out at the worst times – and always carry a map and compass as back up.

Mobile Phones

Mobile phone reception is at best iffy in the hills so it's definitely best not to rely on it. If you do need to make contact with emergency services, try heading up towards higher ground, where you often have more chance of a signal.

Footpaths and rights of way

The walks in this book all follow rights of way, permissive paths or cross open access land.

Comfort

A decent pair of boots will protect your feet from the kind of terrain experienced in the hills and will also provide ankle support, waterproofing and grip on steep slopes. Waterproof jackets and trousers could be useful on any day, at any time of year. A pack containing waterproofs, spare layers and some food and drink, will make your day more comfortable. Trekking poles are a definite asset since they provide greater stability and security on steep ground or slippery footpaths, thereby lessening the chances of an accident resulting from difficult terrain.

Safety

Mountain weather changes quickly and unexpectedly. If you are in any doubt, it's probably best not to start, and if you do get caught out, it's always better to back off your route rather than carry on regardless. The mountains will always be there. In winter, consider carrying a torch in case the light fades before you get off the hill – it's difficult reading a map in the dark.

Mountain Rescue

In case of an emergency dial **999** and ask for **Police** and then **Mountain Rescue**. When possible give a 6-figure grid reference of your location or that of the casualty. If you don't have reception where you are, try and attract the help of others around you. The usual distress signal is six short blasts on a whistle every minute. If you don't have a whistle then shouting may work.

Mountain Rescue by SMS Text

Another option in the UK is contacting the emergency services by SMS text – useful if you have a low battery or intermittent signal, but you do need to register your phone first. To register, simply text **'register'** to 999 and then follow the instructions in the reply. Do it now – it could save yours or someone else's life. **www.emergencysms.org.uk**

The Countryside Code

Be safe – plan ahead

Even when going out locally, it's best to get the latest information about where and when you can go; for example, your rights to go onto some areas of open land may be restricted while work is carried out, for safety reasons or during breeding and shooting seasons. Follow advice and local signs, and be prepared for the unexpected.

- Refer to up-to-date maps or guidebooks.
- You're responsible for your own safety and for others in your care, so be prepared for changes in weather and other events.
- There are many organisations offering specific advice on equipment and safety, or contact visitor information centres and libraries for a list of outdoor recreation groups.
- Check weather forecasts before you leave, and don't be afraid to turn back.
- Part of the appeal of the countryside is that you can get away from it all. You may not see anyone for hours and there are many places without clear mobile phone signals, so let someone else know where you're going and when you expect to return.

Leave gates and property as you find them

Please respect the working life of the countryside, as our actions can affect people's livelihoods, our heritage, and the safety and welfare of animals and ourselves.

- A farmer will normally leave a gate closed to keep livestock in, but may sometimes leave it open so they can reach food and water. Leave gates as you find them or follow instructions on signs; if walking in a group, make sure the last person knows how to leave the gates.
- In fields where crops are growing, follow the paths wherever possible.
- Use gates and stiles wherever possible – climbing over walls, hedges and fences can damage them and increase the risk of farm animals escaping.
- Our heritage belongs to all of us – be careful not to disturb ruins and historic sites.
- Leave machinery and livestock alone – don't interfere with animals even if you think they're in distress. Try to alert the farmer instead.

Protect plants and animals, and take your litter home

We have a responsibility to protect our countryside now and for future generation so make sure you don't harm animals, birds, plants or trees.

» Litter and leftover food doesn't just spoil the beauty of the countryside, it can be dangerous to wildlife and farm animals and can spread disease – so take your litter home with you. Dropping litter and dumping rubbish are criminal offences.
» Discover the beauty of the natural environment and take special care not to damage, destroy or remove features such as rocks, plants and trees. They provide homes and food for wildlife, and add to everybody's enjoyment of the countryside.
» Wild animals and farm animals can behave unpredictably if you get too close, especially if they're with their young – so give them plenty of space.
» Fires can be as devastating to wildlife and habitats as they are to people and property – so be careful not to drop a match or smouldering cigarette at any time of the year. Sometimes, controlled fires are used to manage vegetation, particularly on heaths and moors between October and early April, so please check that a fire is not supervised before calling 999.

Keep dogs under close control

The countryside is a great place to exercise dogs, but it is the owner's duty to mak sure their dog is not a danger or nuisance to farm animals, wildlife or other people

» By law, you must control your dog so that it does not disturb or scare farm animals or wildlife. You must keep your dog on a short lead on most areas of open country and common land between 1 March and 31 July, and at all times near farm animals.
» You do not have to put your dog on a lead on public paths as long as it is under close contro But as a general rule, keep your dog on a lead if you cannot rely on its obedience. By law, farmers are entitled to destroy a dog that injures or worries their animals.
» If a farm animal chases you and your dog, it is safer to let your dog off the lead – don't risk getting hurt by trying to protect it.
» Take particular care that your dog doesn't scare sheep and lambs or wander where it might disturb birds that nest on the ground and other wildlife – eggs and young will soon die without protection from their parents.
» Everyone knows how unpleasant dog mess is and it can cause infections – so always clean up after your dog and get rid of the mess responsibly. Also make sure your dog is wormed regularly.

Consider other people

Showing consideration and respect for other people makes the countryside a pleasant environment for everyone – at home, at work and at leisure.

» Busy traffic on small country roads can be unpleasant and dangerous to local people, visitors and wildlife – so slow down and, where possible, leave your vehicle at home, consider sharing lifts and use alternatives such as public transport or cycling. For public transport information, phone Traveline on 0871 200 2233.
» Respect the needs of local people – for example, don't block gateways, driveways or other entry points with your vehicle.
» By law, cyclists must give way to walkers and horse riders on bridleways.
» Keep out of the way when farm animals are being gathered or moved and follow directions from the farmer.
» Support the rural economy – for example, buy your supplies from local shops.

How to use this book

This book should provide you with all of the information that you need for an enjoyable, trouble free and successful walk. The following tips should also be of help:

1. We strongly recommend that you invest in the Ordnance Survey maps listed on page ix. These are essential even if you are familiar with the area – you may need to cut short the walk or take an alternative route.

2. Choose your route. Consider the time you have available and the abilities/level of experience of all of members your party – then read the safety section of this guide.

3. We recommend that you study the route description carefully before setting off. Cross-reference this to your OS map so that you've got a good sense of general orientation in case you need an escape route. Make sure that you are familiar with the symbols used on the maps.

4. Get out there and get walking!

Maps, Descriptions, Distances

While every effort has been made to maintain accuracy within the maps and descriptions in this guide, we have had to process a vast amount of information and we are unable to guarantee that every single detail is correct.

Please exercise caution if a direction appears at odds with the route on the map. If in doubt a comparison between the route, the description and a quick cross-reference to your OS map (along with a bit of common sense) should help ensure that you're on the right track. Note that distances have been measured off the map, and map distances rarely coincide 100% with distances on the ground. Please treat stated distances as a guideline only.

Ordnance Survey maps are the most commonly used, are easy to read and many people are happy using them. If you're not familiar with OS maps and are unsure of what the symbols mean, you can download a free OS 1:25,000 map legend from **www.v-outdoor.co.uk**

Here are a few of the symbols and abbreviations we use on the maps and in our directions:

 ROUTE STARTING POINT   **ROUTE MARKER**    **OPTIONAL ROUTE**

 ADDITIONAL GRID LINE NUMBERS TO AID NAVIGATION

PB = public bridleway; **PF** = public footpath; **GR** = grid reference.

Km/mile conversion chart

Metric to Imperial

1 kilometre [km]	1000 m	0.6214 mile
1 metre [m]	100 cm	1.0936 yd
1 centimetre [cm]	10 mm	0.3937 in
1 millimetre [mm]		0.03937 in

Imperial to Metric

1 mile	1760 yd	1.6093 km
1 yard [yd]	3 ft	0.9144 m
1 foot [ft]	12 in	0.3048 m
1 inch [in]		2.54 cm

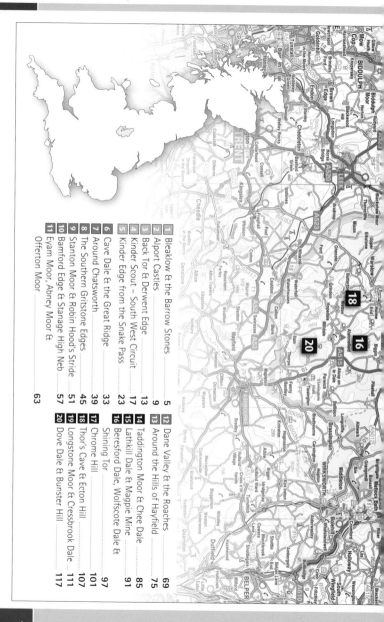

Day Walks in the
PeakDistrict
Area Map & Route Finder

CONTAINS ORDNANCE SURVEY DATA © CROWN COPYRIGHT AND DATABASE RIGHT

SECTION 1

The High Moors

The walks in this category are located in the northern part of the Peak District. This is an area of bleak yet beckoning heather-clad moors, the habitat of red grouse, curlew and golden plover. It has remote crags, impressive deeply cut valleys, down which flow tumbling mountain streams with waterfalls and inviting pools. It is also a land of man-made forests and reservoirs that, if anything, enhance the beauty of this upland landscape.

EDALE AND GRINDSBROOK CLOUGH (ROUTE 4) *PHOTO: JOHN COEFIELD*

1

HOWDEN MOORS IN WINTER (ROUTE 3) PHOTO: JON BARTON

GRINAH STONES PHOTO: JOHN COEFIELD

Bleaklow & the Barrow Stones

15km/9.4miles

A walk in wild moorland to a remote corner of Bleaklow and the source of the River Derwent.

King's Tree » Black Dike » Round Hill » Barrow Stones » Humber Knolls » Slippery Stones » King's Tree

Start

King's Tree, Upper Derwent Valley. Cars and parking only permitted on week-days. Access to King's Tree by bus from Fairholmes car park at weekends and Bank Holidays. GR: SK 167938.

The Walk

Our route follows a steep forest track that leads us from the starting point up to open ground on a broad ridge. An easy trod gradually ascends within or alongside a dyke and the route crosses a track coming up from the Westend Valley. The ground is usually wet underfoot until it steepens and the path climbs Round Hill, where a wind-break of stones is well placed.

The last part of the climb, still straightfor-ward, continues up to Barrow Stones.

This remote spot boasts some magnificent panoramas, highlighted by distant land-marks. From Barrow Stones, a diversion to the rocky promontory at Grinah Stones is well worth the extra kilometre or so it adds to the route.

The route leads past fascinating, wildly var-ied, weather-sculpted blocks of gritstone. 800m of pathless descent lead us to the infant Derwent, which is but a meandering stream at this point. A trod then leads to a footpath that descends alongside the maturing stream as it drops over little waterfalls, forming pools that are tempting on a hot day. The path can be boggy in parts, but is generally straightforward. Our walk finishes along a track that leads us back, via Slippery Stones, to King's Tree.

BLEAKLOW & THE BARROW STONES

DISTANCE: 15KM/9.4MILES » **TOTAL ASCENT:** 430M/1,420FT » **START GR:** SK 167938 » **TIME:** ALLOW 5–5½ HOURS
MAP: OS EXPLORER OL1 DARK PEAK, 1:25000 » **REFRESHMENTS:** NONE ON ROUTE, SHOP AT FAIRHOLMES
NAVIGATION: PROFICIENCY IN MAP-READING AND COMPASS SKILLS NEEDED

Directions — Bleaklow & the Barrow Stones

➊ From King's Tree walk back along the road for 700m to the prominent right-hand bend

➋ Turn up the track on the **right** and follow this up steeply to a gate at the top of the wood

➌ Bear half left up the moorland meadow. The path soon becomes more obvious as it ascends parallel to a broken wall. Keep **straight on** as the path enters the dike. Follow the dike. At one point there is a **rightward** kink, after which it is better to follow the trod on its left side. Eventually a line of posts leads to the vehicle turning point on the track from the Westend Valley.

➍ Either **turn right** on the paved path, then **turn left** in 50m, or walk **north** on a footpath, passing pools to join the latter further on. After a wet section, the path steepens as it **bears right** and climbs to a windbreak on Round Hill and **bears left** up to Barrow Stones.

> **OR** For Grinah Stones follow the trod to the **left** for 600m, then retrace your steps.

➎ A choice of trods leads **right** to more outlying stones. At the northern edge of the rocks, descend to a newly constructed fence. The stile is out of sight, just to the right. Cross this, walk **left** to the point where you met the fence. From here, walking on a bearing of **30° magnetic**, use a combination of trods, groughs and a grass slope to descend. After the angle eases, keep on the right of a shallow valley to avoid wet areas. Continue to the stream, which is narrow and easy to step across hereabouts.

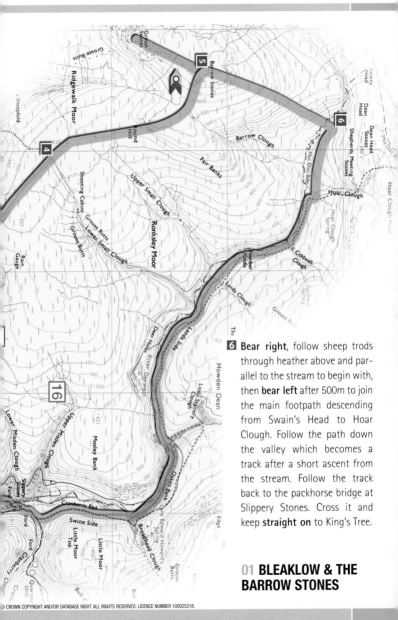

6 **Bear right**, follow sheep trods through heather above and parallel to the stream to begin with, then **bear left** after 500m to join the main footpath descending from Swain's Head to Hoar Clough. Follow the path down the valley which becomes a track after a short ascent from the stream. Follow the track back to the packhorse bridge at Slippery Stones. Cross it and keep **straight on** to King's Tree.

01 BLEAKLOW & THE BARROW STONES

ALPORT CASTLES PHOTO: JON BARTON

Alport Castles

15.3km/9.5miles

This varied walk takes in lakeside, forest and open moor, and has the remarkable landslip feature known as Alport Castles as its focal point.

Fairholmes » Bridgend » Lockerbrook Heights » Alport Castles » Alport » Roman road » Rowlee ridge » Lockerbrook Heights » Fairholmes

Start

Fairholmes car park, Upper Derwent Valley. GR: SK 172893.

The Walk

The route starts by following a path that takes us through woods alongside Lady-bower reservoir for a kilometre. It joins an ancient bridleway that leads up through forest to high, open pastures on a broad ridge. We have uninterrupted views from the ridge, across to Kinder Scout, the Great Ridge and the Vale of Edale.

Our route gradually ascends the broad ridge for 4km, to a sensational viewpoint above the naturally formed, but quarry-like, craggy landscape of the landslip known as Alport Castles. Some of the topographical features within this landslip bear some resemblance to castle ruins.

From this airy spot above the deep, narrow valley of Alport Dale the route descends to the isolated hamlet of Alport. To avoid any road walking, the route then follows a track that leads to the A57, crossing the road and the River Ashop. It continues along a short section of the Roman road before re-crossing the river and the road. A track then leads us uphill to Lockerbrook, and our route ends with a descent along a forest path that heads directly back to Fairholmes.

ALPORT CASTLES

DISTANCE: 15.3KM/9.5MILES » **TOTAL ASCENT:** 589M/1,933FT » **START GR:** SK 172893 » **TIME:** ALLOW 5–5½ HOURS
MAP: OS EXPLORER OL1 DARK PEAK, 1:25000 » **REFRESHMENTS:** NONE ON ROUTE, SHOP AT FAIRHOLMES
NAVIGATION: STRAIGHTFORWARD ON CLEAR PATHS AND TRACKS.

Directions – Alport Castles

➎ From the car park walk back to the road, **turn left** and continue to Overlook car park. **Bear left** along a path between the road and the reservoir to Bridgend car park (about a kilometre).

2 Take the bridleway track that leads up through the forest from the edge of the car park.

3 On emerging on a ridge at the forest edge, **turn right** and follow the path, with the forest on the right, to where it joins a gravel track after a stile or gate at a right-hand bend. **Cross** the track and continue **straight ahead** uphill to a ladder stile. Keep **straight on**. The path becomes paved for about 1.5km, then reverts to a spongy, wet footpath as it approaches Alport Castles. Continue as far as the remains of a wall that lies, oddly, at right angles to the cliff edge (viewpoint).

4 Retrace your steps for 500m, then **bear right** along a footpath descending into Alport Dale. This descends quite steeply to a footbridge over the River Alport. **Bear right** after the bridge and continue up to Alport.

5 Follow the track down to the A57, bearing downhill to the **left** along a footpath just before reaching Hayridge Farm. This leads to Alport Bridge. Cross the road and go down the track opposite via a gate to cross the River Ashop at a ford – usually not more than a few centimetres deep except in very wet conditions. Stay on the track, which climbs to a gate and junction with another track (Roman road). **Turn left**, follow the Roman road for 300m, then take a **left fork** downhill. This leads back across the river and goes up to the A57.

6 Cross the road and continue uphill past Rowlee Farm along another track. Follow it to a fork at a left-hand bend, then **bear left** down to Lockerbrook Outdoor Centre. Carry on along the track for a further 250m.

7 Cross the stile on the right and follow the waymarked path into woodland and downhill. On joining a track turn **right**. Continue round a left hand hairpin and in a short distance turn **right** to take the concessionary footpath back down to Fairholmes.

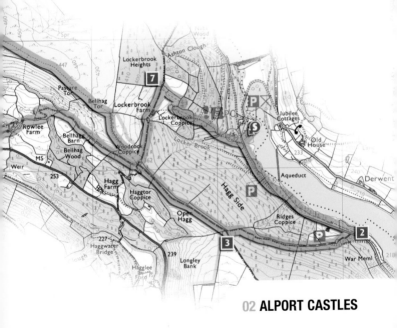

02 ALPORT CASTLES

VIEW SOUTH ALONG DERWENT EDGE FROM BACK TOR PHOTO: JOHN COEFIELD

03 Back Tor & Derwent Edge

17km/10.6miles

, varied walk on clear footpaths, with stunning valley and upland scenery.

airholmes (Upper Derwent) » Abbey Brook » Lost Lad » Back Tor » Derwent Edge » Whinstone
e Tor » Ladybower Reservoir » Fairholmes

Start

airholmes car park below the Derwent
am in the Upper Derwent Valley.
R: SK 172893.

The Walk

his route follows a track along the tree-
ned shore of the Derwent Reservoir, near-
 as far as Howden Dam. A short, steep pull
ads to easier ground, where a gradually
scending footpath takes us through the
eep, winding valley of Abbey Brook. This
loses in to form an impressive steep-sided
orge in its upper reaches, with spectacular
andslip features.

t this point, our route escapes from the
onfines of the gorge along a path that
ads out on to open moorland and onward
 the cairn on the rounded hill at Lost Lad.

A short stretch along a paved footpath
affords us an easy route to Back Tor, a gritstone outcrop on Derwent Edge and the
highest point on the walk. This is a place to
savour the panorama that extends in all
directions. A descending path now takes
our route south along Derwent Edge. Along
the way, it passes other tors and the fascinating weathered rock features known as
the Cakes of Bread, the Salt Cellar and the
Coach and Horses – all aptly named.

All too soon, it is time to descend by means
of a bridleway to the banks of Ladybower
Reservoir. On the last leg, our route passes
the site of the drowned village of Derwent.

BACK TOR & DERWENT EDGE

DISTANCE: 17KM/10.6MILES » **TOTAL ASCENT:** 430M/1,400FT » **START GR:** SK 172893 » **TIME:** ALLOW 5-6 HOURS
MAP: OS EXPLORER OL1 DARK PEAK, 1:25000 » **REFRESHMENTS:** SHOP AT FAIRHOLMES » **NAVIGATION:** ALTHOUGH
CLEAR FOOTPATHS ARE USED THROUGHOUT, PROFICIENCY IN MAP AND COMPASS SKILLS IS RECOMMENDED.

Directions – Back Tor & Derwent Edge

1 Walk below the Derwent Dam and climb steps beside the right-hand tower to join the track on the east side of the Derwent Reservoir. **Turn left** and follow this for just over 2km to the second signposted footpath on the right (Ewden).

2 **Bear right** off the track and follow the path up, taking a **left fork** after the initial steep section. Continue along the gradually ascending footpath, which keeps parallel with the brook. After 2km, prominent landslips form a spectacular feature within the gorge. At the same point, Sheepfold Clough joins on the right.

3 Take a **right fork** and follow a footpath up the clough and out of the gorge on to open moorland. Continue to a paved footpath.

4 **Turn left** and follow this up to the cairn at Lost Lad, then continue for a further 500m to Back Tor.

5 **Turn right** and follow the path along Derwent Edge for nearly 4km, to the second footpath crossroads.

> ⊗ *SC: **Turning right** at the first footpath crossroads would lead to the bridleway described below in **6** and shorten the route by 1.5km.

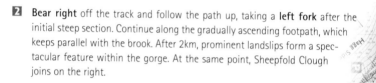

Turn right on the bridleway and follow it downhill. Pass **left** through a gateway after 1km, and keep **straight on** down past Grindle Barn to the banks of Ladybower.

Turn right and follow the lane back to Fairholmes, passing the site of Derwent Village en route.

03 BACK TOR & DERWENT EDGE

STREAM NEAR JACOB'S LADDER PHOTO: JON BARTON

This walk has a mountain character, using an old packhorse route in ascent, then it follows high-level path, to take in some incredible natural rock features and stunning scenery long the way.

dale » Barber Booth » Upper Booth » Jacob's Ladder » Swine's Back » Crowden Tower » Ringing oger » Edale

Start

dale pay and display. GR: SK 124853.

The Walk

rom Edale, our route follows a path across elds to the hamlet of Barber Booth and on o Upper Booth. The Old Norse term 'booth' efers to summer pastures.

track leads us past a wood turner's cot-age, continuing to the packhorse bridge at ne foot of Jacob's Ladder. We follow the aved footpath that heads straight up the illside, making for the saddle at Edale ross. Alternatively, the old bridlepath takes less direct approach to gain height.

ur climb from the saddle continues a little urther. The going becomes easier as we each the high-level path that follows the dge of the summit plateau. The undulating ootpath passes two rock features, shown on the map as Noe Stool and Pym Chair, then takes us into the amazing area of eroded rocks, known as the Wool Packs. Some of these do resemble wool packs, but some are more like giant mushrooms or chess pieces, whilst others are more animalistic in their features.

A little further on, Crowden Tower, a tall gritstone crag, dominates Crowden Clough. A stretch of paved footpath leads us to the craggy cirque of Grindsbrook Clough over-looking Edale. The path clings to the rim of the cirque, offering ever-changing views, as we progress across the tops of crags, or 'tors'. The route off the top takes us down one of the lesser-known footpaths, that takes a more gradual line than most. We follow a series of gradually descending zigzags back to the valley bottom and on to Edale to end our walk.

KINDER SCOUT – SOUTH WEST CIRCUIT

DISTANCE: 15.6KM/9.7MILES » **TOTAL ASCENT:** 570M/1,870FT » **START GR:** SK 124853 » **TIME:** ALLOW 6 HOURS
MAP: OS EXPLORER OL1 DARK PEAK, 1:25000 » **REFRESHMENTS:** NONE ON ROUTE. PUBS AND A CAFÉ IN EDALE.
NAVIGATION: ALTHOUGH THE PATHS USED ARE CLEAR TO FOLLOW, AMBIGUITIES AND ROUTE FINDING DIFFICULTIES COULD BE
EXPERIENCED IN MISTY OR WINTRY CONDITIONS. SKILLS IN THE USE OF MAP AND COMPASS ARE THEREFORE ADVISABLE.

Directions – Kinder Scout – South West Circuit

⑤➤ Leave the car park, passing the toilets, and walk up the road towards Edale village. At the first right-hand bend, **turn left** (fingerpost) and head for a handgate. Continue along the obvious foot-path. Pass below a farm, cross a track, and **bear half left** down a field. Continue to a railway bridge, cross it and enter Barber Booth.

2 **Keep right** in the hamlet, passing a chapel, join a track and cross the rail-way again. **Turn left** and follow the obvious path across fields to the farm at Upper Booth, where you **turn left** to join the lane. **Turn right** and follow the lane/track to a footbridge at the foot of Jacob's Ladder. Use the paved footpath or take the more gradually ascending bridlepath up the hillside. Continue climbing fairly steeply, until you reach a short, level section with a resting place.

3 Take the **right fork** off the main footpath. This soon joins a path that climbs from the saddle between Brown Knoll and Kinder Scout. Continue uphill to where it levels out near the rocks of Swine's Back. The path climbs gently to Noe Stool, and continues to the rocky outcrop at the back of which is Pym Chair. From here the path, or rather multiplicity of paths, passes through the Wool Packs, The easiest of these skirts the rocks on the north side. If the weather conditions deteriorate at this point, **head due east**. Continue another 250m or so to Crowden Tower on the right of the footpath and overlooking the deeply incised valley of Crowden Clough.

DIRECTIONS CONTINUE OVERLEAF ▷

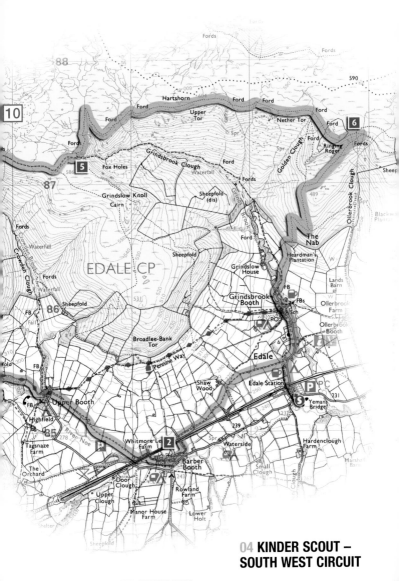

04 KINDER SCOUT –
SOUTH WEST CIRCUIT

4 Descend, with difficulty, the steep gravelly path, then cross the brook. An easier option is to **bear left** and follow a footpath that heads back into the wilderness of the plateau crossing two streams before returning to the edge footpath, having bypassed the difficult stretches. Continue along the edge footpath, later stretches of which are paved. At a fork adjacent to prominent stones go **left** along the paving stones. This leads to the top of the craggy cirque of Grindsbrook Clough.

5 **Turn left**. Keep to the edge footpath. This makes a 500m detour, first to the north, then south, as it crosses the top of a crag-lined gully before it can head eastwards. Continue along the obvious path, often paved, and staying close to the edge. This is much easier and less erosive than wading through peaty sections further left. The path climbs a little as it passes above Upper Tor, then continues across the top of Nether Tor. 300m further on is the top of Golden Clough, with footpaths leading steeply downhill. Ignore these and take the higher level of two footpaths. This reaches a protected enclosure above the rocks of Ringing Roger. **Bear half left** after crossing the stile to emerge in 150m at another stile.

6 Continue **left** for 100m, then take the narrow path that doubles back downhill below Ringing Roger (difficult to make out until you are in line with it). Continue to a path junction, then **turn left**. Take the next rightward option to zigzag down The Nab. This becomes paved. Continue down to the valley bottom, **bearing left** to pick up the path that crosses the river and enters Edale. Keep **straight on** to reach the car park.

FAIR BROOK PHOTO: JON BARTON

raggy, steep-sided slopes, tumbling streams, remote gritstone crags and long-distance
ews over wild country give this route the atmosphere and character of a mountain walk.
rchen Clough » Fair Brook » Fairbrook Naze » Kinder Edge » Ashop Head » Ashop Clough »
rchen Clough

Start

irchen Clough lay-by 1km up the A57
rom the Snake Pass Inn. GR: SK 109914.

The Walk

ur route follows the footpath that leads up
o the Kinder Plateau. It takes us through
he gorge etched out by Fair Brook, a
nountain stream with waterfalls and deep,
lear pools. The path is awkward in parts,
specially the last half kilometre, which
limbs steeply. The best way up this section
. to stay close to the stream.

he path along the rim of the plateau con-
nues north to the promontory at Fairbrook
laze. There are exceptionally fine views of
ne deep valleys and surrounding high
noors. We follow an obvious but sinuous
ath in a westerly direction across the top
f The Edge. It weaves its way over and
round eroded rocks and boulders, and
cross peaty sections. The best choice of
oute here is always near the rocks at the
dge of the crag.

Our route eventually joins the Pennine Way
footpath. A 3km diversion allows us to see
the spectacular craggy amphitheatre of
Kinder Downfall. The descent uses the
Snake Path, which follows Ashop Clough.
The stream and the path share the same
course for a short section, but fortunately,
this does not last for long and the path
soon improves. The gorge deepens and the
stream becomes a river. Our path clings to
the steep valley side as it descends to the
Snake Pass and the end of our walk.

KINDER EDGE FROM THE SNAKE PASS

DISTANCE: 14KM/8.75MILES » **TOTAL ASCENT:** 560M/1,835FT » **START GR:** SK 109914 » **TIME:** ALLOW 5–6 HOURS
» **MAP:** OS EXPLORER OL1 DARK PEAK, 1:25000 » **REFRESHMENTS:** SNAKE PASS INN » **NAVIGATION:** PROFICIENCY IN MAP-
READING AND COMPASS SKILLS NEEDED.

Directions – Kinder Edge from the Snake Pass

❻ From Birchen Clough cross the main road and descend steps to reach the riverside footpath, then **turn left**. Cross a track and stay on the riverside path. On passing through a gate, **bear left**. The path soon ascends to the A57. **Turn right** and follow the roadside path to the Snake Pass Inn. Opposite the car park, cross a stile on the right. Continue through the wood below the main road, eventually **bearing right** down to cross the River Ashop by the footbridge.

2 Follow the path above the River Ashop then **bear right** into the valley of Fair Brook. The path climbs parallel with the brook for most of its two kilometre length to reach the plateau. The best way to tackle the last steep section is to stay on the immediate right of the stream as it tumbles over the rocks, ignoring the temptation to move to higher possibilities which would prove to be more difficult.

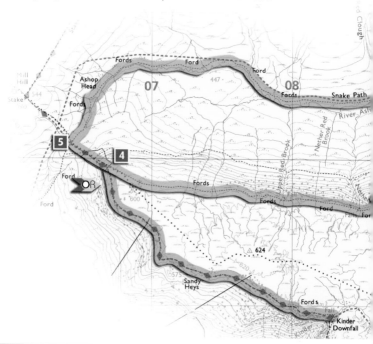

3 **Turn right** at the top and follow the indefinite path along the rim of the plateau to the promontory at Fairbrook Naze. The path now **turns west** and follows the top of The Edge for just over 2km, where the rim of the plateau now turns southeast. This joins the Pennine Way.

DIRECTIONS CONTINUE OVERLEAF

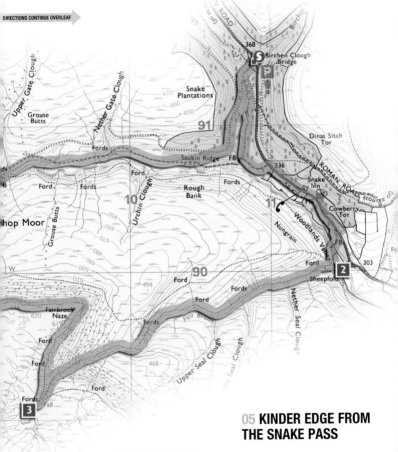

05 KINDER EDGE FROM THE SNAKE PASS

Directions – Kinder Edge from the Snake Pass continued...

▶OR▶ If you have the time and inclination, **turn left** on the Pennine Way and walk fc 1.5km to the Downfall, then retrace your steps.

4 **Turn right** to continue west along the Pennine Way footpath. After a steep descer on inlaid stones the path reaches a junction at Ashop Head.

5 **Turn right** and take the Snake Path down Ashop Clough. The first part is paved, bu this does not last for long, and a wet section has to be negotiated for a short distanc before the path improves. About 4km from Ashop Head the path enters a plantatior At a waymark post with white markings, **bear left**. Follow the waymarked patl through the wood and up to a forest track. This descends to cross the River Ashop **Turn left** and retrace the outward route, heading up to the right in 100m.

PHOTO: JON BARTON

SECTION 2

Hills, Tors & Edges

The area in which the walks in this category fall is located to the south of the high moors and includes the eastern and western borderlands of the Peak District. Here the landscape is characterised by broad ridges, with hilltops, gritstone tors and escarpments with craggy edges. This is a varied landscape of wooded river valleys and 'cloughs', wild meadows, pasture and scattered farmsteads, of lower lying moors with stone circles and other ancient relics.

THE GREAT RIDGE FROM MAM TOR (ROUTE 6) PHOTO: JOHN COEFIELD

CAVE DALE, PEVERIL CASTLE AND LOSE HILL PHOTO: JOHN COEFIELD

06 **Cave Dale** & the **Great Ridge**   15.2km/9.5miles

This exhilarating walk combines riverside, a limestone gorge and a ridge with three prominent summits and fine views.

Hope » Castleton » Cave Dale » Windy Knoll » Mam Tor » Lose Hill » Hope

Start

Hope. Village car park or roadside.
GR: SK 171835.

The Walk

Our route follows a riverside path to Castleton. We follow the narrow limestone gorge of Cave Dale that leads steeply uphill to the high pastures above the village. Level walking along tracks provides a breather before we climb to the summit of Mam Tor.

The route passes a cave at Windy Knoll. When this site was excavated by archaeologists, it yielded various prehistoric artefacts that suggest that the cave was used as a temporary shelter by nomadic Stone Age hunter-gatherers. Mam Tor was the site of an Iron Age hill fort and the ramparts and other earthworks are still clearly discernible. The summit is a prime viewpoint and its popularity with tourists has made it necessary to lay setts to prevent further erosion of the hillside.

Our route now descends to the ancient crossing point at Hollins Cross before climbing Back Tor. After another dip in the ridge the path climbs to Lose Hill summit, another splendid viewpoint. We finish by descending to Hope through fields.

CAVE DALE & THE GREAT RIDGE

DISTANCE: 15.2KM/9.5MILES » **TOTAL ASCENT:** 580M/1,890FT » **START GR:** SK 171835 » **TIME:** ALLOW 5½ HOURS
MAP: OS EXPLORER OL1 DARK PEAK, 1:25000 » **REFRESHMENTS:** LOTS OF CAFÉS AND PUBS IN HOPE AND CASTLETON
NAVIGATION: STRAIGHTFORWARD.

Directions – Cave Dale & the Great Ridge

➔ Turn down the road to Pin Dale by the Woodroffe Arms. Continue over the bridge and up to a stile on the **right**.

2 Cross this and follow the riverside footpath. This leads to Castleton, crossing a railway track en route.

3 **Turn left** on joining the main road. Walk as far as the Nag's Head at the second right-angled bend. Continue up to the **left** of the hotel along Back Street. Carry on past the old market square and **bear left** on the minor road. In a short distance, **turn right** to enter Cave Dale (signposted).

4 Follow the steepening path up through the narrow gorge. **Bear right** through a bridlegate, and continue more easily through fields to arrive at a gate with stile.

5 **Turn right**, pass through another gate, then continue along the track. Keep **straight on** at the fork. Follow the track uphill for 600m to a stile on the right just before a gate.

DIRECTIONS CONTINUE OVERLEAF

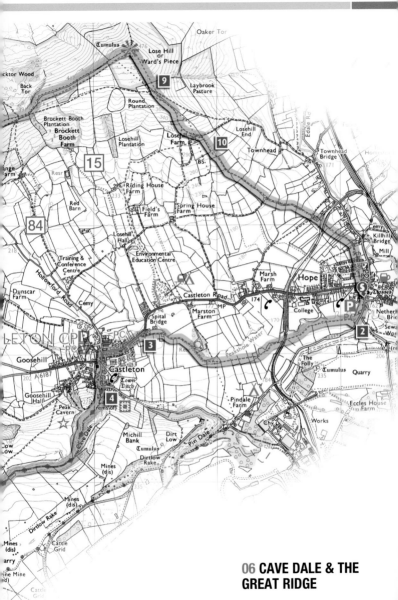

06 CAVE DALE & THE GREAT RIDGE

Directions – Cave Dale & the Great Ridge continued…

6   Cross the stile and follow the path with a wall on the left. After two stiles, the path descends to a gate and the main road.

7   Cross the road, go through the gate opposite and keep **straight on** with a wall on the left. (Windy Knoll and the cave are to the right of the path.) On arriving at another road, cross it and the handgate opposite, then follow the ascending path up to a stile at Mam Nick.

8   **Bear right** along the paved path that climbs to the summit of Mam Tor. Continue along the undulating ridge via Hollins Cross and Back Tor for 3.5km to the summit of Lose Hill. Continue down the other side to a stile. Cross it, then take a **right fork**.

9   After crossing another stile in a few metres, **turn sharp left** to follow a path down to farm buildings.

10   Just left of the farm, cross a stile **on the right**, then keep **straight on** downhill exiting the second field by a stile **on the left**. Continue along the obvious path. Keep a straight course to emerge opposite the Woodroffe Arms.

Around Chatsworth   18km/11miles

A walk through an incredible mix of man-made and natural landscape, that includes hill pastures, woodland, lakes, open moor and riverside.

Calton Lees » Calton Houses » Ballcross Farm » Edensor » Chatsworth House » Hunting Tower » Beeley Moor » Beeley » Calton Lees

Start

Calton Lees picnic area in Chatsworth Park on the B6012 1.6km south of Chatsworth House. GR: SK 258685.

The Walk

From the justly popular riverside pastures at Calton Lees in Chatsworth Park, a gradual climb on tracks and field paths leads us to the sheep pastures above the valley, and on to a viewpoint overlooking the hills and valleys west of Baslow.

Our route now descends to the estate village of Edensor. Designed by Joseph Paxton, the original village, sited nearer the house, was demolished and rebuilt in its present form in the 1830s. Queen Mary's Bower is just a short walk away. It dates from the 16th Century and may have been used by Mary Queen of Scots during her incarceration at Chatsworth in the 1570s.

The climb from the river takes us past Chatsworth House and the Farmyard, then continues steeply up the delightful wooded hillside. We visit the broken aqueduct and waterfall en route to the Hunting Tower, built as a summer house for Bess of Hardwick in the 16th Century. On from here, a forest track leads us round past Emperor and Swiss Lakes. Outside the park, the landscape changes abruptly to open moorland with views across the river valley.

We descend to the estate village of Beeley, then stroll across riverside meadows to round off a varied outing.

AROUND CHATSWORTH

DISTANCE: 18KM/11MILES » **TOTAL ASCENT:** 468M/1,537FT » **START GR:** SK 258685 » **TIME:** ALLOW 5–5½ HOURS **MAP:** OS EXPLORER OL24 WHITE PEAK, 1:25000 » **REFRESHMENTS:** TEASHOP AT EDENSOR. STABLES TEASHOP AT CHATSWORTH HOUSE. DEVONSHIRE ARMS AT BEELEY. » **NAVIGATION:** STRAIGHTFORWARD.

Directions – Around Chatsworth

⮕ Follow the road that passes above the garden centre, then bends right into a valley Keep **straight on** through a gate and along the track uphill to Calton Houses. Continu past the cottages and through a bridlegate.

2 **Turn left** and stay parallel with the wall on the **left**, then go left through a gat between woods. **Bear slightly left** and ascend the hillside – posts guide the way – t the edge of a walled plantation.

DIRECTIONS CONTINUE OVERLEAF ▸

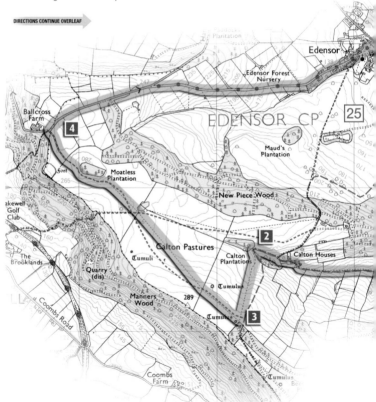

Parkgate

CHATSWORTH CP

Chatsworth
Park
(Deer Park)

26

Queen Mary's
Bower

Chatsworth
House

The Hunting
Tower

7

5

27

Stand
Wood

Swiss
Lake

Swiss
Cottage

6

The Willow
(Fountain)

FB

112

FB

The
Grotto

Bunker's Hill
Wood

234

Park
Farm

276

8

Weir

106

Old Park
Plantation

Weir

Rabbit Warren

Stone Circle

Enclosure

on Lees

Bridge

Beeley
Lodge

Beeley
Hilltop

9

Rounds

277

Waterfalls

207

Hell Bank
Plantation

10

Beeley

07 **AROUND CHATSWORTH**

Directions – Around Chatsworth continued...

3   Instead of going through the wood, **turn right** and follow the field path as it firs contours then gradually descends to the left side of a pond. Keep **straight on** an **pass just left** of a wooded knoll. A track is soon joined which leads to a lane.

4   **Turn right**. Follow the lane over the hilltop then downhill to where a track **forks righ** off the lane. Follow this downhill to and through Edensor. Cross the main road, then tak the gravel path opposite. This leads to a bridge. Cross it and walk up and past Chats worth House. **Pass left** of The Stables and approach the Farmyard after a cattle gri

5   Follow the tarmac lane uphill past the Farmyard. Take the path **bearing uphill to th left**, signposted *The Dell*. Cross a lane and continue uphill along the path that passe beneath the broken aqueduct. Stay on the right of the tumbling stream and carry o up to the top of the waterfalls.

6   Descend the steps on the other side, then stay on the path that contours the hillside **Ignore** further steps that descend to the left. Eventually, the path emerges at th Hunting Tower.

7   **Turn right** facing the Tower and walk along a path to a track. Follow this, **ignorin** any rightward options. The track winds round past Emperor and Swiss Lakes and afte 2km reaches a crossroads. Go **straight across**. Stay on the track, which soon **bear left** to a gate and stile.

8   Keep **straight on** along the track for about 1.5km, to where it ends at a gate and stile Cross the stile and **turn right** to follow the track downhill for another 1.5km to Beele Hilltop Farm.

9   **Turn left** at the fingerpost/stile. **Bear right** across the farmyard and go through a gate Keep **straight on** with a wall on the left, then maintain the same course downhil Follow the obvious field path via stiles into Beeley.

10   **Turn left**, then **right** by the church. Cross the main road and go through the gat opposite. Follow the path across the field to the road bridge. After crossing this, tur **right** through a gate to walk alongside the river, then **bear left** before the ruin up t the road and the car park.

CURBAR EDGE FROM BASLOW EDGE PHOTO: JOHN COEFIELD

08 The Southern Gritstone Edges

18.5km/11.5miles

High level footpaths, continuously changing views and impressive crags characterise this walk along the southern gritstone edges.

Baslow » Baslow Edge » Curbar Edge » Froggatt Edge » Grouse Inn » White Edge » Gardom's Edge Chatsworth Edge » Baslow

Start

Baslow. The walk is described from the pay and display car park. GR: SK 258721.

The Walk

From Baslow, a track leads us uphill to Wellington's Monument on Baslow Edge. The 'Gritstone Edges' form an escarpment, two-tiered for some of its length. From these abrupt sandstone crags, so popular with climbers, the slope descends gently eastwards.

In its outward journey, our route follows paths north along the top of Baslow, Curbar and Froggatt Edges, then climbs slightly higher to the overlying escarpment of White Edge. The path along here leads us south, then continues along the top of the much less frequented Gardom's Edge. We also take in Chatsworth Edge, before finally descending through Chatsworth Park to finish.

The views along the way justify the popularity of these cragtop footpaths, although some sections along White Edge can be muddy after wet weather. A short exposed section of footpath along the top of Chatsworth Edge can be a problem for those that suffer from vertigo, but this can be avoided by taking a lower-level footpath.

Deer can often be sighted in Chatsworth Park – an added bonus on this route.

THE SOUTHERN GRITSTONE EDGES

DISTANCE: 18.5KM/11.5MILES **» TOTAL ASCENT:** 500M/1,660FT **» START GR:** SK 258721 **» TIME:** ALLOW 6 HOURS
MAP: OS EXPLORER OL24 WHITE PEAK, 1:25000 **» REFRESHMENTS:** THE GROUSE INN AT THE HALFWAY MARK AND THE
ROBIN HOOD INN 2.5KM FROM THE END **» NAVIGATION:** STRAIGHTFORWARD ON WELL-USED PATHS.

Directions – The Southern Gritstone Edges

⑤ Cross the main road at the pelican lights and **bear left** up Eaton Hill. **Turn right** School Lane and continue uphill along a road, then track, to Wellington's Monumen

2 **Retrace your steps** for a short distance then **bear right** and follow the broad pat – or a narrower footpath along the top of Baslow Edge (optional route) – to the roa at Curbar Gap. Cross the road, go through a gate and keep **straight on** along a broa path above Curbar Edge. The path continues above Froggatt Edge, eventually emerg ing at a main road.

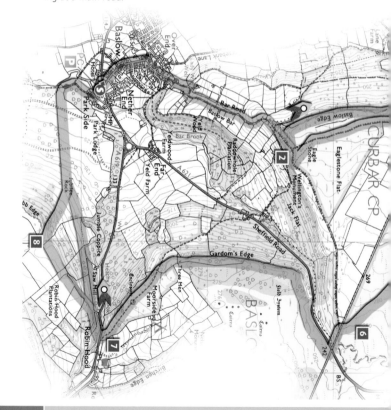

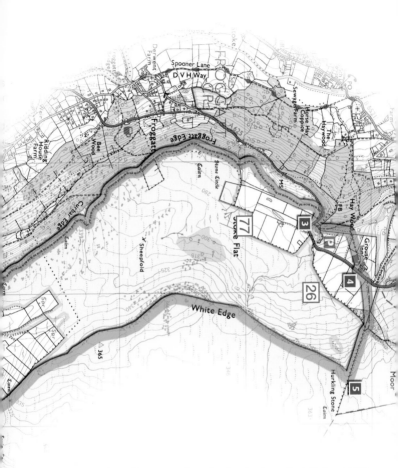

3 **Turn right** and, in a short distance, go through a hand-gate on the left. Descend to cross a stream and go up to Hay Wood car park. Keep **straight on** across and past the car park to reach a stile in the wall on the right. Cross it and continue across fields to rejoin the main road, just below the Grouse Inn.

DIRECTIONS CONTINUE OVERLEAF ▶

08 THE SOUTHERN GRITSTONE EDGES

Directions – The Southern Gritstone Edges continued...

4   Pass the inn, then cross the road to a gate. Follow the path up to a path junction. **Bea right** and follow the path with a wall on the right to a path crossroads.

5   **Turn right**. Follow the path along the top of White Edge for 3km. Shortly after th path begins to descend, the more well-used path descends steeply to the right. Instea keep **straight on** along the less well-defined path to emerge near a road junction.

6   **Turn left**, continue to the road junction, then cross the main road and the gate o the **right**. **Bear right** to follow the path that runs more or less parallel to the roa Keep **straight on** through a handgate and continue in the same direction into th woodland above the crags of Gardom's Edge. Instead of following the often mudd and tortuous path by the wall on the left, make for the top of the crags, where th going is much easier and more pleasant with great views of the Derwent Valley belo Eventually you are forced back to the wall on the left, which leads down to a gatewa Once through this follow one of several options in the same general direction pa Moorside Rocks and down to the main road.

7   Cross the main road to a stile almost opposite, then descend stone steps, cross a foo bridge, and continue up to a track.* Cross this, continue over a ladder stile and follo the concessionary path along the top of Chatsworth Edge. A rail protects a sho exposed section. The path descends a little after the crags peter out, crossing tw stiles, then climbs again to resume its former course.

> ***** **OR** The path along the top of Chatsworth Edge is exposed over a short sectio This can be avoided by **turning right** along the track to walk under the crag and enter Chatsworth Park at a lower level. Should this option be taken, o entering the Park continue in the same general direction as the track just use

8   After crossing a high stone stile, **turn right** and descend through Chatsworth Par **bearing half left** away from the boundary wall on the right, initially using an o grassed-over quarry track. There are stiles across a wooden fence at regular interva to permit access to the tarmac drive. Cross this, aim for the left edge of a wood, an continue to a junction with a prominent footpath. **Turn right**, pass through a turn stile then continue into Baslow.

09 Stanton Moor & Robin Hood's Stride

15km/9.4miles

This route combines wild, unspoilt woodland, open moor full of archaeological relics, a gritstone tor, a hermit's cave, and three lovely villages.

Winster » Cowley Knowl » Stanton Moor » Birchover » Robin Hood's Stride » Elton » Winster

Start

Winster. Park in the car park at the eastern end of the village. GR: SK 246606.

The Walk

The village of Winster was established in ancient times. The Domesday Survey, commissioned by William the Conqueror in 1085, lists 'Winsterne' as a village of twenty dwellings. Although the architecture is of interest generally, it is the 16th Century Market Hall that is the real gem. The village expanded in the 18th Century as a result of the lead mining industry.

Not far into our walk, the ruin of an engine house at Cowley Knowl testifies to the area's industrial heritage. The section from Winster to Birchover follows paths through a stretch of unspoilt woodland, before climbing to Stanton Moor.

Here we see a total contrast in vegetation – now mainly open heather moor with a scant covering of birch. The moor is littered with excavated Bronze Age burial mounds and we visit the stone circle known as Nine Ladies.

After circumnavigating the moor, our descent takes in the old quarry village of Birchover. We continue from here along a combination of tracks and field paths on the approach to the gritstone tor of Robin Hood's Stride. Cratcliffe Tor can be found nearby. At its foot, we find the Hermit's Cave, notable for the 12th Century crucifix carved into the rock.

More field paths, a stroll down a quiet lane, then a short, sharp climb, lead us to Elton, an attractive village of stone cottages. We finish off by following the Limestone Way back to Winster.

STANTON MOOR & ROBIN HOOD'S STRIDE

DISTANCE: 15KM/9.4MILES » **TOTAL ASCENT:** 340M/1,100FT » **START GR:** SK 246606 » **TIME:** ALLOW 5 HOURS
MAP: OS EXPLORER OL24 WHITE PEAK, 1:25000 » **REFRESHMENTS:** RED LION AND DRUID INN AT BIRCHOVER. DUKE OF YORK AND A CAFÉ AT ELTON. MINER'S STANDARD AND OLD BOWLING GREEN AT WINSTER » **NAVIGATION:** STRAIGHTFORWARD.

Directions – Stanton Moor & Robin Hood's Stride

➜ **Turn right** out of the car park. Walk down the road for 150m and cross the stile on the left. **Bear right** across fields with stiles. At two stile posts (no fence), **bear slightly left** to the bottom corner of the field and a stile hidden from view at first. Continue along the woodland path. On emerging from the wood **bear left** up a track to a gate/barrier.

2 **Turn left** on the path before the gate, pass in front of the engine house ruin and then continue on the woodland path. This eventually joins a track. **Turn left** and follow the track for 500m to a finger-post/stile on the right.

3 Cross this and keep **straight on** up through fields, through Barn Farm as waymarked and up to a road.

4 **Turn right** and take the first path on the left. Pass the information board then **fork right** and continue to the stile at Stanton Moor Edge. Stay on the left of the fence and continue up to join a higher level path. Follow this around the moor, passing left of the tower folly, to the Nine Ladies Stone Circle. Pass left of the circle and continue to a path crossroads at a corner of a fence.

DIRECTIONS CONTINUE OVERLEAF ▷

09 STANTON MOOR & ROBIN HOOD'S STRIDE

Directions – Stanton Moor & Robin Hood's Stride continued...

5   Turn **left** and at the next path crossroads, **left** again. The path passes right of the triangulation pillar and arrives at the Cork Stone. **Turn right** and walk down to the road.

6   Turn **left**. 300m along the road **turn right** opposite the stone factory and follow the descending path to the road opposite the Druid Inn. (Alternatively, stay on the road to walk through the village to the inn.) Cross the road. Take the lane along the left side of the inn. Stay on this, which becomes a gravel track, then follow the old walled track around the hill. At the second gate, again keep **straight on**. After a stile, descend through a field and climb to the main road right of a house. Cross the road and continue on the path to other houses.

7   Turn **right** and go down the lane. Keep **straight on** through a handgate on the left of a gate (Limestone Way). Follow the track uphill. Keep **straight on** where this bends right to where the path levels out adjacent to Robin Hood's Stride.* Cross the stile on the left, then that in the wall on the right. Follow the path across two fields to a road.

     *⟩**OR**⟩ Halfway up this section a stile in the wall to the right of the path gives access to a path to the foot of Cratcliffe Tor at the south end of which is the Hermit's Cave. To regain the route, retrace your steps for 50m, cross a stone stile adjacent to the wooden one crossed earlier, then **bear half right** aiming for the prominent rocks of Robin Hood's Stride.

8   Turn **left**. Follow the lane for a kilometre to a prominent right-hand bend, then cross the stile on the left (fingerpost on right showing the way). Follow the obvious path through fields first in descent, then uphill to Elton. On meeting a lane **bear right**, then **right** again up to Main Street.

9   Turn **left**. Walk through the village and continue along the road to a track on the right (Limestone Way) opposite Dudwood Lane. **Turn right** and follow the track, crossing a lane, and continue uphill to emerge at a road.

10   Turn **left**. Continue across a junction, then follow Ease Bank down into Winster. **Turn right** to finish.

NINE STONES CLOSE STONE CIRCLE, HARTHILL MOOR PHOTO: JOHN COEFIELD

10 Bamford Edge & Stanage High Neb

16.7km/10.4miles

A walk with outstanding views, passing over the tranquil heights of Bamford Edge and the more remote northern crags of Stanage Edge.

Hollin Bank » Bole Hill » Bamford Edge » Cutthroat Bridge » Moscar » Stanage Edge » Hollin Bank

Start

Hollin Bank picnic area/car park below Stanage Edge, 3km north of Hathersage. GR: SK 238837.

The Walk

Footpaths through fields and woodland lead us across the upper reaches of two stunning valleys that descend to join the Hope Valley below. Our walk enters the access land of Bamford Moor, following an old overgrown quarry track to Bamford Edge. The path runs along the top of the crags that overlook Ladybower Dam and Reservoir. The views from hereabouts are breathtaking!

The path beyond the crags narrows for a short distance as it clings to the edge of the slope and takes us through heather and bilberry. After we cross two broken-down walls, the ground levels out. There is a pre-historic hut circle to the right of the path.

A gradual descent around the hillside on a little-used but discernible path leads us to Cutthroat Bridge. Two kilometres of ascending footpath and track takes us on to the path that runs the length of Stanage Edge. A gradual climb leads past old quarry workings and across the top of the more remote northern crags. Here we reach the highest point on the walk at High Neb.

After three kilometres along Stanage Edge, our route ends by descending to the car park along an ancient, paved trail, formerly used by packhorses.

BAMFORD EDGE & STANAGE HIGH NEB

DISTANCE: 16.7KM/10.4MILES » **TOTAL ASCENT:** 570M/1,870FT » **START GR:** SK 238837 » **TIME:** ALLOW 5½–6 HOURS
MAP: OS EXPLORER OL1, DARK PEAK, 1:25000 » **REFRESHMENTS:** OCCASIONAL SNACK/COFFEE VAN IN CAR PARK
NAVIGATION: DEMANDS CONCENTRATION FOR A SHORT DISTANCE BEYOND THE CRAGS OF BAMFORD EDGE.

Directions – Bamford Edge & Stanage High Neb

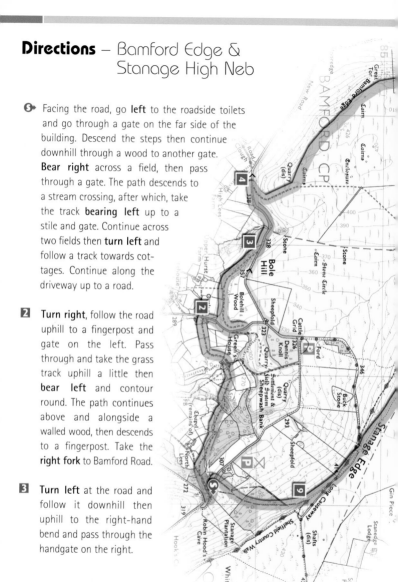

➏ Facing the road, go **left** to the roadside toilets and go through a gate on the far side of the building. Descend the steps then continue downhill through a wood to another gate. **Bear right** across a field, then pass through a gate. The path descends to a stream crossing, after which, take the track **bearing left** up to a stile and gate. Continue across two fields then **turn left** and follow a track towards cottages. Continue along the driveway up to a road.

2 **Turn right**, follow the road uphill to a fingerpost and gate on the left. Pass through and take the grass track uphill a little then **bear left** and contour round. The path continues above and alongside a walled wood, then descends to a fingerpost. Take the **right fork** to Bamford Road.

3 **Turn left** at the road and follow it downhill then uphill to the right-hand bend and pass through the handgate on the right.

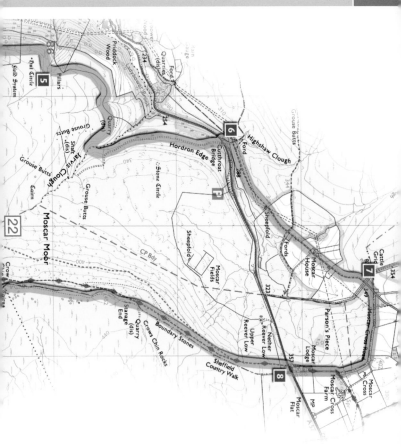

4 Take the path **forking right**. This climbs gradually to a disused quarry. Use the path that skirts around it on the right then **bear left** above the quarry. The path heads for the edge of the escarpment, with a steep slope down to the left. **Keep to the left** so that you follow the path that runs along the top of Bamford Edge. Where the crags end, stay on this narrow footpath as it clings to the top of the steep slope overlooking Ladybower Dam. The path runs through heather and bilberry then cuts back into a gully, where you cross a stream.

DIRECTIONS CONTINUE OVERLEAF ▶

10 BAMFORD EDGE & STANAGE HIGH NEB

Directions – Bamford Edge & Stanage High Neb continued...

5 Make for the corner of a high wall straight ahead with a small rock outcrop directly behind it on the uphill side. Walk above and parallel with this wall as it **bears right** around the hillside. Where the wall turns to descend to the left at a tiny disused quarry with a solitary pine, follow the path as it **bears right** and downhill. Take the most gradually descending path to a stream crossing, ignoring the first steep and muddy option. Go up then **bear left** to join a track. Follow the track down to the A57 at Cutthroat Bridge.

6 Cross the road, go through the gate opposite, then follow the path up beside the stream for 50m only. **Bear right** to cross the stream below, then keep **straight on** along the ascending path. Stay on this course, pass Moscar House and emerge at a road.

7 Cross over and follow the road opposite for 100m, then **turn right** through a gate. Walk uphill and pass though two more gates. Follow the track as it bears right downhill, then **bear right** through a gate to keep **straight on** downhill to the A57.

8 **Turn right**, then cross the stile on the left. Follow the path uphill to a disused quarry and the first crags of Stanage Edge. Take the path that runs along the top of the crags. Pass the triangulation pillar at High Neb and continue to a junction with a stony track.

9 Cross this and continue above the rocks for another 150m, then **bear right** downhill along the old packhorse route. The route soon becomes a paved path that leads back to the car park.

LADYBOWER RESERVOIR AND BAMFORD EDGE PHOTO: JOHN COEFIELD 61

VIEW TOWARDS BRETTON CLOUGH FROM HUCKLOW EDGE   PHOTO: JOHN COEFIELD

11 Eyam Moor, Abney Moor & Offerton Moor

18.8km/11.7miles

This walk takes the high ground to the west of Hathersage, offering fine views of the area, and includes open moorland, woodland and riverside.

Hathersage » Leadmill » Eyam Moor » Sir William Hill » Bretton » Hucklow Edge » Abney Grange » Abney Moor » Offerton » Leadmill » Hathersage

Start

Hathersage pay and display car park.
GR: SK 231814.

The Walk

On leaving Hathersage, a path across riverside meadows leads us to a crossing of the River Derwent. This is where our climb begins in earnest, first along a lane, then on a footpath up the flanks of Eyam Moor. The ascent continues up to the summit of Sir William Hill.

The walk then takes on a more undulating character, passing a cottage in Nether Bretton that sits in an enviable position overlooking Bretton Clough, with Hathersage and the gritstone tors and edges beyond. When Bonnie Prince Charlie's marauding Jacobite army passed through these parts in 1745, Bretton Clough provided local people with a hiding place for their livestock .

A little further on is the Barrel Inn, which dates from 1637. A favourite haunt of lead miners through the centuries, it also lay on the 'salt trail' from Cheshire to the Yorkshire towns. Our route continues along a lane that keeps to the crest of Hucklow Edge. This offers views to the north of the hills and moors of the gritstone or 'Dark' Peak, and, to the south, of the limestone country known as the 'White' Peak. After passing a gliding club, the route takes a path across open moor, from which there is an unusual, distant, end-on view of Ladybower.

Another path leads us across the flanks and over the top of Offerton Moor, then descends to 16th Century Offerton Hall Farm. A mixture of tracks, field and woodland paths sustains interest en route back to the riverside meadows of the Derwent. The last few metres of descent are muddy and slippery in wet conditions, making trekking poles a useful accessory.

EYAM MOOR, ABNEY MOOR & OFFERTON MOOR

DISTANCE: 18.8KM/11.7MILES » **TOTAL ASCENT:** 530M/1,745FT » **START GR:** SK 231814 » **TIME:** ALLOW 5–5½ HOURS **MAP:** OS EXPLORER OL1 DARK PEAK, 1:25000, OS EXPLORER OL24, WHITE PEAK, 1:25000 » **REFRESHMENTS:** BARREL INN AT BRETTON, OUTSIDE CAFÉ HATHERSAGE » **NAVIGATION:** STRAIGHTFORWARD ON WELL USED FOOTPATHS THROUGHOUT.

Directions – Eyam Moor, Abney Moor & Offerton Moor

➊ With your back to the car park, **turn right** and walk down to the junction. **Turn left**, then cross the road and take the first **right**. Follow the lane under the railway and on to a gate/stile on the **left**. Cross this and follow the obvious path to emerge at the main road.

2 **Turn right** and cross the bridge. Continue along the pavement and take the second road on the **right**. Follow this uphill, or take the parallel path on the left of the hedge. Continue past Hazelford Hall. The road zigzags then the angle eases as it approaches cottages at Leam. Continue to the stile on the right.

3 Cross the stile and **bear left** uphill. Follow the path up the moorside to emerge at a road in about 1.5km. **Turn right** and follow the track up and over Sir William Hill, passing the prominent mast, to its junction with a road.

DIRECTIONS CONTINUE OVERLEAF

11 EYAM MOOR, ABNEY MOOR & OFFERTON MOOR

Directions – Eyam Moor, Abney Moor & Offerton Moor continued...

4 Go **straight on**, then take the track on the right. Follow this around past Nether Bretton and up into Bretton. **Turn right** and continue along the road, then take a **right fork**. Follow the road along the ridge. After a short descent, take a **right fork**. The road climbs and bends to the right then levels out adjacent to the gliding club landing strip.

5 Go through the handgate on the right and follow the field path as it descends, then crosses a wet gully just right of a building. The path crosses a stile then **bears right** across more fields, before descending to cross another gully. Keep the same course and emerge at the road further on, having cut the corner.

6 **Turn right**, then cross the stile on the **left**, which has a bench on the other side. Follow the path across the moor for 1.5km to a junction with a track.

7 **Turn right**. Follow the track as far as the sharp left-hand bend, then keep **straight on** before **bearing right** to follow the path that skirts the hillside to the right. This contours above a wall at first, then descends a little. Where the wall heads downhill to the right, keep **straight on** and reach a footpath crossroads. **Turn left** here. Follow the path over the moor then downhill to the lane adjacent to Offerton Hall Farm. (The exit stile is down to the left).

8 **Turn right** and continue along the lane for 400m, then cross a stile on the **left. Bear right**. The path eventually emerges at Callow Farm. **Turn left** and cross the stile to the left of the cottage facing. Continue downhill and through a wood to emerge at a track.

9 **Turn right** and continue up the track, then cross a stile on the **left** in 200m. Follow the descending path to the riverside, the last few metres requiring care in wet conditions. **Turn right** and continue to Leadmill Bridge. **Turn left**, cross the bridge, then **turn left** at the stile and retrace your steps to Hathersage.

2 Dane Valley & The Roaches   19.5km/12miles

tough but exhilarating outing, taking in a wooded river gorge, the ridgelike crest of a
ritstone escarpment, a nature reserve and heather-clad moorland.

adbach » Danebridge » Hangingstone » Roach End » The Roaches » Naychurch » Ramshaw
cks » Gib Tor » Gradbach

Start

radbach, riverside car park and picnic
rea, 4.5km west of the A53 midway
etween Buxton and Leek, and 3km east
f the A54, Buxton to Congleton road.
ollow the road for the Youth Hostel.
R: SJ 998662.

he Walk

rom the remote setting of Gradbach in the
ane Valley, we follow a winding woodland
ath above the river as it descends through
gorge. Indigenous trees such as oak, birch
nd ash, and the bilberry beneath them,
resent a wild countenance.

n arriving at the hamlet of Danebridge the
imbing starts, and soon our route joins
e crest of the long escarpment that forms
e gritstone crags of The Roaches. It weaves
s way amongst the weathered rocks above
e crags and the highest point on the walk
ffers us extensive views of the Stafford-
hire countryside. The route then descends
a break in the escarpment, beyond which
e the soaring crags of Hen Cloud.

Some interesting route-finding follows,
where the right of way is not always
obvious, but the stiles are all in place. Soon
the path begins the climb along the ridge of
Ramshaw Rocks, whose jutting, jagged,
overhanging rocks serve as a distinctive
landmark. Further on, after a short descent
through heather, the rocky escarpment
leads into Black Brook Nature Reserve. Rare
bog plants native to this area thrive in its
wet climate. From here, lanes, old tracks
and field paths lead us through the
welcoming final descent.

DANE VALLEY & THE ROACHES

ISTANCE: 19.5KM/12MILES » **TOTAL ASCENT:** 570M/1,870FT » **START GR:** SK 998662 » **TIME:** ALLOW 6 HOURS
MAP: OS EXPLORER OL24 WHITE PEAK, 1:25000 » **REFRESHMENTS:** NONE ON ROUTE » **NAVIGATION:** MOSTLY WELL
MARKED PATHS BUT SHORT SECTIONS ON LESS WELL USED PATHS REQUIRE CLOSE ATTENTION TO THE ROUTE DESCRIPTION.

Directions – Dane Valley & The Roaches

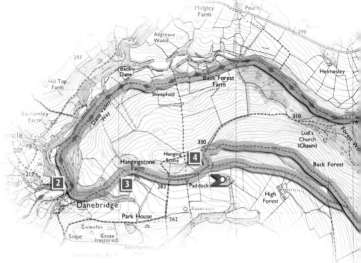

➎ **Turn right** out of the car park, follow the road for 200m, then **bear right** down the drive to the youth hostel. **Pass right** of the hostel. Follow the path, then a track as far as a left-hand bend. Keep **straight on** here, cross a footbridge and continue above the river towards Danebridge. The path climbs away from the river to pass round the back of two dwellings.

2 About 50m before reaching the bridge at Danebridge, **turn left** at the finger post/stile for Hangingstone. Climb steps and follow the waymarked path through a wood, then **bear left** up a field to a track.

3 **Turn right**, follow the track above Hangingstone Farm and below the Hanging Stone to a turning area. **Bear left** up a track to a fingerpost for Gradbach. Continue to a gateway.

4 **Turn left** and ascend the Gradbach path to the ridge, then **turn right** to follow the path along this to Roach End. Alternatively, you can keep **straight on** to Roach End (Optional Route). Cross the road and climb the paved path to the triangulation point on The Roaches. Keep **straight on** along the crest for 1.5km to a path crossroads.

DIRECTIONS CONTINUE OVERLEAF ▶

12 DANE VALLEY & THE ROACHES

Directions – Dane Valley & The Roaches
continued...

5 **Bear left** and descend gradually to a wall that cuts across at right angles. Instead
going through the handgate facing you, walk **left** alongside the wall to another gat
Pass through this then **bear half left**. Pass through two more handgates, then ski
farm buildings to a fingerpost/handgate on the **left**.

6 **Turn right**, follow the track downhill as far as a right-hand bend and gateway.

7 **Bear left** here and walk with a wall on the right, ignoring a stile in that wall, to a sti
and stream. Cross these and go up the walled track that has become part of a garde
Turn right to walk alongside the wall. Continue to a stile, then **bear left** through th
farm and up to the road. **Bear right** to the main road.

8 **Turn left** at the fingerpost to follow the path up through heather to a road. **Turn lef**
and follow the road to a fingerpost on the right. **Turn right** and follow the path u
and along the crest of Ramshaw Rocks. (Easier, less exposed options to the left.) Kee
straight on past the sign *Ramshaw Ridge* to a path junction by a wall.

9 **Turn right**, follow the path for 200m to a fork. **Bear left** with the fence on your righ
On reaching a stile on the right, **turn left** to follow the path that descends oblique
through heather. Continue across a stile, keep **straight on** to another on the left, the
take the best line across the boggy field to a stile opposite a cottage.

10 Cross the road, **pass right** of the cottage and follow the path beside more rocks. Ente
a nature reserve, then keep a straight course until a fingerpost is reached. Walk **righ**
as directed, skirting the boggy ground, Continue through a wood to a road.

11 **Turn left**, follow the road up and round to the left, then downhill. Keep **straight o**
at road junctions then go up the walled track. This ends at a handgate. Keep **straigh**
on staying close to the wall on the left. Cross to the other side of this when the goin
is easier on the far side. Continue downhill, pass piles of all sorts and descend to
gate and track. **Bear right**. Stay on this track as it becomes a tarmac lane leading bac
to the car park.

BOSLEY CLOUD FROM THE ROACHES PHOTO: JOHN COEFIELD

VIEW ACROSS COLDWELL CLOUGH TO KINDER PHOTO: JON BARTON

3 **Around** the **Hills** of **Hayfield**

13.5km/8.4miles

Stunning views and several climbs on bridlepaths characterise this walk amongst the hilly terrain around Hayfield Village.

Bowden Bridge » Peep O Day » Chinley Churn » Lantern Pike » Middle Moor » Bowden Bridge

Start

Bowden Bridge pay and display car park on Kinder Road, a kilometre east of Hayfield village. GR: SK 048869.

The Walk

From Bowden Bridge, where the Rivers Kinder and Sett meet, a bridleway leads us up steeply to a col on the flanks of Mount Famine. The views, both on the climb and from the col, are quite breathtaking.

The route resumes, climbing along a track that brings us to the top of the broad ridge of Chinley Churn, with its discarded quarry workings and abandoned stone walls. From here, a two kilometre descent, from which there are distant views of Kinder Reservoir, leads us to Birch Vale. The route crosses the Sett Valley Trail, then starts to climb once more along the Pennine Bridleway.

We follow the bridleway up to Lantern Pike. A diversion along a footpath takes us to the summit, which affords panoramic views of Black Hill to the north, Kinder Scout to the east, Mount Famine and South Head to the south and the Cheshire Plain to the west.

The descent leads us to Little Hayfield, then the last climb takes us up the outlying flanks of Kinder Scout. We follow a narrow path through rhododendrons, bilberry and heather, before joining another bridlepath. A stunning view suddenly presents itself on White Brow overlooking Kinder Reservoir, a man-made phenomenon that enhances the magnificent natural amphitheatre of Kinder's steep western flanks.

The descent follows the bridleway and a quiet lane back to Bowden Bridge to end the walk.

AROUND THE HILLS OF HAYFIELD

DISTANCE: 13.5KM/8.4MILES » **TOTAL ASCENT:** 640M/2,110FT » **START GR:** SK 048869 » **TIME:** ALLOW 5 HOURS **MAP:** OS EXPLORER OL1 DARK PEAK, 1:25000 » **REFRESHMENTS:** LANTERN PIKE INN AT LITTLE HAYFIELD » **NAVIGATION:** STRAIGHTFORWARD.

Directions – Around the Hills of Hayfield

➏ Cross the bridge opposite the car park and follow the road **left**. This bends right, then further on crosses a bridge and climbs. Take the 'Horses and Cycles' route via the gate/stile ahead. Follow the bridleway where it leaves the lane and continue up steeply. After a gate, the path levels out. Cross a broad track and follow another track down to the main road.

2 **Turn left**, then cross to the lane leading **right**. Follow this past Peep O Day Farm and keep **straight on** at the bend through a gate. Stay on the track all the way up the hill to Higher Hills Cottage. Follow its continuation to the gate on the crest of the hillside. Continue now on the level to a track junction and gate.

3 **Turn right** and keep **straight on** along this as it descends, ignoring all other possibilities. Eventually, the main road in Birch Vale is joined. Cross it to a fingerpost and follow the path down to and across the Sett Valley Trail. Continue past an angling pond, cross a footbridge, then **bear slightly right** up to a handgate. Follow the obvious path up to a lane.

4 **Turn left**, follow the lane as it zigzags uphill to a road. Cross this and take the steep lane/bridleway just right of cottages. Continue uphill, past a cottage, and through a gate ahead. Leave the bridleway here and ascend **left** by a wall, then **bear right** to the summit of Lantern Pike. Continue down the other side to rejoin the bridleway just before a gate. Pass through this. The path **bears right** then bends to the left to cross the large field to a fingerpost and bridle gate.

5 **Turn right** before the gate and walk with a wall on the left. The path is vague at first. Continue downhill. On reaching a cottage, cross the drive to a stile and continue the descent, **bearing left** at first. Pass behind the mill conversion and reach a lane. **Turn left** and climb to the main road. (Lantern Pike Inn to the left.)

DIRECTIONS CONTINUE OVERLEAF

13 AROUND THE HILLS OF HAYFIELD

6 Cross the road and follow the unmade road beside Park Hall Woods. After the left-hand bend, go through the gate on the right to access Middle Moor. Follow the narrow footpath straight up the hillside. On joining a bridleway in 500m, **turn left** and follow this to a path junction below a shooting cabin.

7 **Bear right**, then **right again** in 50m to descend the bridleway. Keep **straight on** downhill, pass through a gateway and join a path running alongside the reservoir boundary wall. **Turn right**, follow it steeply down to the reservoir access road, now a concession route, and follow this and the public road back to Bowden Bridge.*

> * OR Alternatively, cross in front of the gate to the reservoir, follow the path across a footbridge, **turn right** to walk alongside the river, then join the road further on.

PHOTO: JON BARTON

SECTION 3

Limestone Country

Walks in this category are located in the central and southern Peak District. They take in spectacular crag-lined limestone gorges with caves, rock pinnacles and scree slopes rich in fossils. They climb to the tops of prominent peaks, once submarine reef knolls in a tropical sea. They cross limestone upland with fascinating relics of past mining industry. And they often pass through quaint villages with Norman churches, old stone cottages and an inviting inn.

WOLFSCOTE DALE (ROUTE 16) **PHOTO:** JOHN COEFIELD

PETER'S STONE IN UPPER CRESSBROOK DALE (ROUTE 19) PHOTO: JOHN COEFIELD

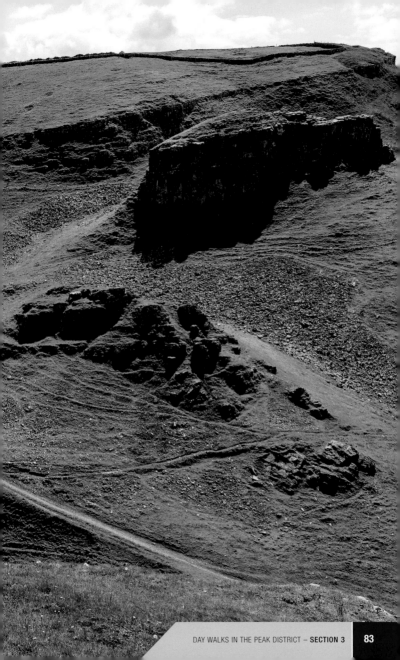

THE RIVER WYE THROUGH CHEE DALE PHOTO: JOHN COEFIELD

14 Taddington Moor & Chee Dale   15.7km/9.8miles

An adventurous excursion that combines rolling limestone upland with an impressive deep river gorge.

Miller's Dale » Priestcliffe » Taddington Moor » Chelmorton » Horseshoe Dale » Deep Dale » Wye Dale » Chee Dale » Miller's Dale

Start

Miller's Dale. Pay and display car park at the former railway station, just off the B6049, 3km south of Tideswell.
GR: SK 138733.

The Walk

We start with a short but steep ascent out of Miller's Dale. This leads us to easier ground, where field paths and country lanes invite us across rolling upland pastures. A further gradual ascent leads us up on to Taddington Moor. This section offers extensive views of the northern White Peak and the high Dark Peak moors beyond.

Our route then begins a long descent, soon passing through the upland village of Chelmorton. Old walled tracks lead us on into the delightful Horseshoe Dale and the secluded gorge of Deep Dale. Here we find Thurst House Cave, whose gaping entrance is a good vantage point for surveying the gorge. The path through Deep Dale is awkward in places but we can avoid most of the difficulties by taking a higher level footpath across scree slopes.

As we enter Chee Dale, we follow the Monsal Trail, the trackbed of a former railway, below some of the most imposing limestone cliffs in the region. We leave the Monsal Trail in favour of the narrow riverside footpath that leads downstream through the main part of the gorge.

Stepping stones allow you to cross and continue where the cliffs abut against the river. These can be impassable during or immediately after wet weather, but there is an alternative route to bypass the problem. Beyond the stepping stones the footpath demands care and concentration for some distance as it climbs above the river, before the going gets easy again.

It would be a good idea to take a trekking pole on this walk.

TADDINGTON MOOR & CHEE DALE

DISTANCE: 15.7KM/9.8MILES » **TOTAL ASCENT:** 470M/1,540FT » **START GR:** SK 138733 » **TIME:** ALLOW 5–6 HOURS **MAP:** OS EXPLORER OL24 WHITE PEAK, 1:25000 » **REFRESHMENTS:** CHURCH HOUSE INN AT CHELMORTON » **NAVIGATION:** STRAIGHTFORWARD.

Directions – Taddington Moor & Chee Dale

5 From Miller's Dale Station, **turn left** along the Monsal Trail, cross the viaduct, then take the second path on the **right** to enter a nature reserve (signposted). Continue up steeply beside a disused quarry, then follow a path across fields. On joining a track **turn left** and emerge at a bend in the road in Priestcliffe.

2 **Bear right** and follow the lane. Keep **straight on** at a crossroads to join the A6 opposite the Waterloo Inn.

3 Cross the road and take the track on the left of the inn. Follow this uphill past the zigzags and continue to where the ground levels out. Pass through a gate. Where there are stiles opposite each other, **turn right**. Continue on the field footpath, cross another track and keep **straight on** down into Chelmorton.

4 Walk past the Church Inn, and keep **straight on** along the village street. After passing Common Lane on the right, **turn right** at the footpath sign. Follow the drive and keep **straight on** through a backyard gate, over a stile, then through fields to a walled track. **Turn left**. Cross a stile straight ahead where the track turns right. **Bear right** to join another track and follow this to a main road. **Bear left**. Where the road bends left, cross a stile straight ahead, then **bear half left**. Cross another stile and keep **straight on** to join the road further on.

DIRECTIONS CONTINUE OVERLEAF

**14 TADDINGTON MOOR
& CHEE DALE**

Directions – Taddington Moor & Chee Dale continued...

5 **Turn right**, follow the road downhill, then **turn right** to enter Horseshoe Dale by gate next to farm buildings. Follow the dale downhill, then its continuation as Dee Dale. Take the higher footpath option across scree slopes. This avoids all but a sho section of potential difficulties underfoot. Exit Deep Dale at Topley Pike Quarry.

6 Cross the A6 into Wye Dale car park. Follow the riverside track downstream. Cross th river at Blackwell Mill Cottages, then continue along the riverside path. Or even bette ascend to the Monsal Trail (signposted). Follow this below towering cliffs to the sec ond exit on the left, then descend to the riverside footpath. Continue downstrean footbridges and stepping stones enabling further progress where the cliffs abut th river.* Continue to the end of Chee Dale, then double back up to the left to Miller Dale Station (signposted).

*⬦OR⬦ If the river is in spate and the riverside path is under water use the Monsal Trai passing through the tunnels, to get back to Miller's Dale Station car park.

THE MONSAL TRAIL THROUGH CHEE DALE PHOTO: JOHN COEFIELD

MAGPIE MINE PHOTO: JOHN COEFIELD

5 Lathkill Dale & Magpie Mine
15.8km/9.8miles

he first half is across rolling limestone upland with extensive views, then the character
f the walk changes dramatically, as one descends a craggy limestone gorge.

ver Haddon » Magpie Mine » Monyash » Lathkill Dale » Conksbury Bridge » Over Haddon

Start

ver Haddon. Pay and display car park at
he west end of the village.
R: SK 203664.

The Walk

rom the attractive upland village of Over
addon, our route follows field paths
cross rolling limestone upland with exten-
ve views of the area. The view we get
hen we arrive at the long-abandoned site
f Magshaw Mine is stunning! The ground
rops away below us into a valley, and ris-
ng on the opposite side are parallel lines of
white stone walls which draw the eye
owards the stark chimney and ruins of
lagpie Mine at Sheldon.

nis, our next objective, is fascinating to
xplore. There is a replica horse gin of the
ype that was used to raise lead ore to the
urface before the installation of a coal-
owered Cornish beam engine.

We leave the mine and descend field paths
towards Monyash. All of a sudden, we are
treated to views of the church tower of this
former mining village in its sheltered, sleepy
hollow. The café and the pub next door
provide a choice of refreshment.

Just outside the village, our route enters
Lathkill Dale. The dale soon narrows and the
path becomes rocky, requiring care. The going
soon improves as we descend the crag-
lined gorge. The stream becomes a river and
enters a heavily wooded section with more
relics of the lead mining industry. Bateman's
House is worth a visit. It lies on the opposite
side of the river and is accessible by a footbridge. As the gorge widens, the river passes
over several attractive weirs as it heads for
the ancient bridge at Conksbury. The route
now doubles back to provide great views of
the gorge as it climbs gradually to Over
Haddon and the end of our trip.

LATHKILL DALE & MAGPIE MINE

DISTANCE: 15.8KM/9.8MILES » TOTAL ASCENT: 370M/1,220FT » START GR: SK 203664 » TIME: ALLOW 5 HOURS
MAP: OS EXPLORER OL24 WHITE PEAK, 1:25000 » REFRESHMENTS: BULLS HEAD PUB AND A CAFÉ AT MONYASH
NAVIGATION: STRAIGHTFORWARD.

Directions – Lathkill Dale & Magpie Mine

❻ **Turn left** out of the car park and walk to the junction with Monyash Road. **Turn left** and follow the road for 300m to a fingerpost/stile on the right, adjacent to a farm shed. **Turn right** to follow the obvious path via stiles to a road. Cross this and the stile opposite, then keep going in the same direction across more fields. The path climbs to a high point with evidence of past mine workings in the vicinity.

2 Cross the stile on the **right**, then another on the **left** in a few metres to pass through a narrow copse. Continue downhill to a stile by a gate. Cross the road and ascend the old walled track opposite. Continue to a fingerpost.

3 **Bear half right**, cross a stile, continue to a path junction in the middle of the field, then turn **left** and continue via a stile to the ruins of Magpie Mine.

4 **Bear right** between the ruins to a stile with fingerpost. Beyond this is another stile, after which **bear slightly left**. Go through an open gateway then **bear right** through another. Now head for the twin wooden pylons, then continue to a stile by a gate to join a road.

DIRECTIONS CONTINUE OVERLEAF

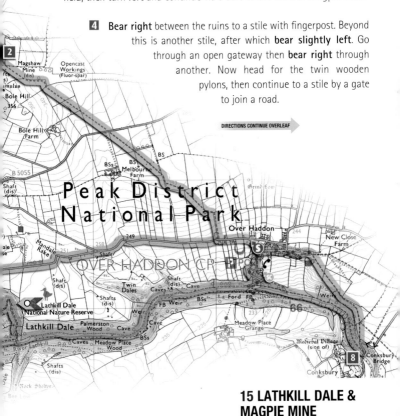

15 LATHKILL DALE & MAGPIE MINE

Directions – Lathkill Dale & Magpie Mine continued...

5 **Turn right**. Follow the road uphill and past a junction, then cross the stile with finger post on the left. Follow the obvious field path through a copse and several field finally **bearing half left** to a stile by a gate to arrive at Horse Lane.

6 **Turn right** and follow the road downhill to a T-junction. **Turn left** and walk up to th crossroads in Monyash. **Turn left** and walk through the village. Follow the road dow to the entrance to Lathkill Dale on the **right**.

7 Follow the path down the gorge for over 5km to an assortment of buildings with road end, a ford and a footbridge.* (Shortcut: an escape to Over Haddon can be mad at this point by climbing the steep winding lane to the left). Continue downstream still on the left bank, for another kilometre to emerge at Conksbury Bridge.

  * **OR** The concession path is closed on Wednesdays from October to Januar which would necessitate the following **Optional Route**: **Turn left** where th way is barred and follow the old winding miner's track up out of the gorge Mill Farm and the road. **Turn right** and follow the road back to Over Haddo

8 **Turn left**, continue up to the elbow of the bend in the road, then cross the stile o the **left**. Follow the footpath along the top of the wooded valley side. In about 400 the path **bears right** uphill away from the rim of the gorge to Over Haddon, emergin opposite the Lathkill Hotel. Walk past the front of the hotel and keep **straight on** t reach the car park.

WOODLAND PATH THROUGH LATHKILL DALE PHOTO: JON BARTON

WOLFSCOTE DALE PHOTO: JOHN COEFIELD

16 Beresford Dale, Wolfscote Dale & Shining Tor

15.4km/9.6miles

This walk follows a path alongside the River Dove, through continuously changing gorge scenery, then climbs out to hill country, passing through a handsome upland village.

Hartington » Wolfscote Dale » Shining Tor » Milldale » Alstonefield » Narrowdale » Beresford Dale Hartington

Start

Hartington, about 19km southeast of Buxton. The walk is described from the market square. GR: SK 128605.

The Walk

After a short climb out of the old market village of Hartington, our route descends to join the River Dove as it enters Wolfscote Dale. We follow a well-trodden path alongside the winding river, as it flows through the narrow gorge it has etched into the limestone plateau. Occasional crags create picturesque scenes. In parts, the path is hemmed in between steep scree slopes and the river, whilst in others, it traverses wide, flat and inviting grassy areas. After passing through riverside woods Wolfscote Dale ends and our route takes to the heights of Shining Tor above Mill Dale, a short kink in the gorge that forms the link with Dove Dale.

Our climb out of the dale is rewarded with views up Wolfscote Dale. After a walk in the open, the path descends to cross the little packhorse bridge at Milldale. We then climb the lane leading to the fine upland village of Alstonefield, with its ancient church, quaint stone cottages and welcoming old inn. Our journey from here uses paths and tracks to make a gradual descent to the Dove once more, where we enter Beresford Dale. The riverside path heads upstream through a heavily wooded gorge with a rock spire rising from a pool. It suddenly emerges into the open for the last kilometre back to Hartington and the end of our outing.

BERESFORD DALE, WOLFSCOTE DALE & SHINING TOR

DISTANCE: 15.4KM/9.6MILES » **TOTAL ASCENT:** 503M/1,652FT » **START GR:** SK 128605 » **TIME:** ALLOW 4¹/₂–5 HOURS
MAP: OS EXPLORER OL24 WHITE PEAK, 1:25000 » **REFRESHMENTS:** THE GEORGE AT ALSTONEFIELD. TEASHOPS AND PUBS IN HARTINGTON. SNACK BAR IN MILLDALE » **NAVIGATION:** STRAIGHTFORWARD.

Directions – Beresford Dale, Wolfscote Dale & Shining Tor

❻ Facing the Devonshire Arms, go **left** then **turn right** up Hall Bank. Take the next road on the **right**, Reynards Lane. Follow this uphill for 800m, then **fork right** up a track to rejoin the lane further on.

2 **Turn right**, follow the lane around a left-hand bend, then cross the stile on the **right** in 100m. **Bear half left** downhill. Continue down an old walled track and across a track junction to reach the riverside footpath.

3 **Turn left**. Follow the path through Wolfscote Dale for about 4km to its junction with the road through Mill Dale.

4 **Turn left**, then cross the road to a handgate and path leading to Shining Tor. Follow this for 300m to the sign for Pinch Bank, then **turn right** and ascend steeply as for Tissington. A path junction is reached at the top of the steep slope. **Turn right**. Follow the path along the rim of the gorge, then descend the zigzag path to cross the packhorse bridge at Milldale hamlet. ⟩OR⟩ (An easier option is to turn **right** and cross the road bridge, then bear **left** and follow the riverside pavement to Milldale.)

5 **Bear left** at the road, then straightaway **turn right** in front of Polly's Cottage and continue up Millway Lane for a kilometre to Alstonefield. On entering the village keep **straight on** and pass in front of The George to reach Lode Lane.

6 **Turn left**, then **bear right** to follow the road out of the village towards Hulme End and Hartington. Continue for 300m beyond the last building to the left-hand bend.

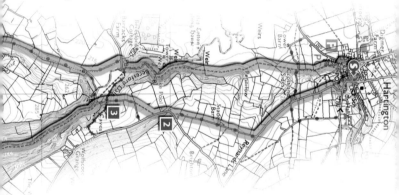

7 Cross the stile with fingerpost on the right, then **bear half left** across fields towards the corner of a small wood. Cross a track and maintain the same general direction across several fields with the ground sloping away to the right. Keep **straight on**, ignoring a stile on the right, and descend to the buildings at Narrowdale.

8 **Turn right** along the track, follow it as it bends to the left and for a further kilometre, where it meets a lane. **Turn right** then take the path on the **left** going upstream alongside the river. Keep **straight on** along this all the way back to Hartington.

16 BERESFORD DALE, WOLFSCOTE DALE & SHINING TOR

17 Chrome Hill

13km/8.25miles

This walk weaves a way through a fascinating area of former reef knolls with distinct peaks, and traverses the fine, narrow limestone ridge of Chrome Hill.

Longnor » Hollinsclough » Fough » Chrome Hill » Dowel Dale » Earl Sterndale » Longnor

Start

Longnor, 13km south of Buxton on the B5053. Park on the square in the village centre. GR: SK 088649.

The Walk

From the old market village of Longnor, a combination of tracks, field paths and quiet country lanes leads us to the hamlet of Hollinsclough, in its sheltered position below the moor. From here we take a bridleway that crosses an ancient packhorse bridge, then gradually ascends a secluded valley. We follow a concessionary path that leads, after a descent and a steep climb, to the start of the ridge of Chrome Hill.

Our walk along the ridge is quite exposed in parts, but easier options avoid obstacles if preferred. We soon reach the summit to enjoy the fine panoramic view.

After descending the steep grass slope from the summit, we follow a quiet lane uphill into Dowel Dale, past a cave used by Stone Age nomads. A short steep path leads us out of the dale then across to the village of Earl Sterndale. Here we can visit the Quiet Woman, a quaint old inn whose sign depicts a headless woman!

The last leg of our walk descends to the Dove Valley to cross the River Dove before a final climb back to Longnor.

CHROME HILL

DISTANCE: 13KM/8.25MILES » **TOTAL ASCENT:** 510M/1,680FT » **START GR:** SK 088649 » **TIME:** ALLOW 4½–5 HOURS **MAP:** OS EXPLORER OL24 WHITE PEAK, 1:25000 » **REFRESHMENTS:** QUIET WOMAN AT EARL STERNDALE. SEVERAL PUBS AND TEASHOP AT LONGNOR » **NAVIGATION:** STRAIGHTFORWARD.

Directions – Chrome Hill

➏ From the square, walk past the Horseshoe Inn then take Gauledge Lane. Follow this to the farm, then cross the squeeze stile on the left opposite the farmhouse. **Bear right** to another stile then keep **straight on**. Ignoring a stile/fingerpost down to the left, **keep a straight course** to reach a half-hidden stile/fingerpost in the wall on the right, and a road.

2 **Turn left** on the road then take the road on the right to Hollinsclough. On reaching the hamlet keep **straight on** past the chapel and up the lane to a bridleway on the right.

3 Follow the bridleway downhill, then across a packhorse bridge. The path climbs steeply to the left to join a track. **Bear left**. Follow the track uphill for a kilometre. Pass over a cattle grid and continue uphill on the lane to a stile on the right next to a gate.

4 Cross this and follow the waymarked route to the left of a fence. Cross a track then follow the waymarked Concession Path to Chrome Hill. This at first keeps **straight on**, then descends to the right, then climbs steeply to reach the start of the ridge. Follow this direct or use easier alternatives to the left or right to gain the summit of Chrome Hill. Descend the grass slope keeping to the left. Cross a stile and continue along the ridge or take a lower level path to reach a lane by a cattle grid.

DIRECTIONS CONTINUE OVERLEAF ▷

17 CHROME HILL

5   **Turn left**, follow the lane up past Dowall Hall Farm to a stile on the right 300m further on from the farm.

6   Cross this and ascend steeply to a stile. Continue parallel with the wall on the left to a stile on the right of a gate. Cross a track and keep **straight on** down the field with a wall on the right to reach a stile on the right. Cross this and follow the track **left** up to the road or cross the stile on the opposite side of the track and **bear half left** up to a stile. **Turn right** at the road, walk down to a junction and go straight across and up into Earl Sterndale.

7   **Turn right** at the Quiet Woman Pub. Pass immediately **right** of the pub and follow the signposted route for Crowdecote. The path climbs through two fields then **bear left** after a stile. Follow the descending path, pass through a handgate and head for the private dwelling and a track.

8   **Turn left** and follow the track. Continue past a farm. 50m past a barn on the right **turn right** at the fingerpost. Cross the wooden stile on the right (not the stone one straight ahead). Keep **straight on**. Cross the River Dove at Beggar's Bridge and continue across fields and a short boggy area. On reaching a barn, **bear left**. Follow the track uphill. **Turn left** at the top, then take the first road on the **right** and work your way down to the village centre.

THE NORTHWEST RIDGE OF CHROME HILL PHOTO: JOHN COEFIELD

18 Thor's Cave & Ecton Hill

13.6km/8.5miles

A walk through and above the Manifold Valley, visiting an impressive cave in a spectacular situation, and a hilltop with a panoramic view.

Hulme End » Wettonmill » Thor's Cave » Wetton » Ecton Hill » Hulme End

Start

Hulme End. Manifold Way car park on the west edge of the village.
GR: SK 102593.

The Walk

We set off along the Manifold Way, a tarmac track that follows the course of the former Manifold Valley Light Railway. Before the tarmac becomes tedious, an interesting track on the opposite side of the river leads to the hamlet at Wettonmill.

A further stretch on the Manifold Way soon reveals views of our next objective: the giant hole in a limestone cliff, aptly known as Thor's Cave. A stiff climb on a paved path leads us to the cave entrance, where we can take in the spectacular surroundings and enjoy an exceptional view up the Manifold. This cave yielded several artefacts dating from Romano-British times.

We follow a more gradually ascending path to the upland village of Wetton. From here, the nature of the walk changes as our route passes through hilly limestone upland, at first descending then climbing to the summit of Ecton Hill for a panoramic view of the area. The rest of our route is all downhill, but it keeps our interest as it passes 18th Century relics and the deep shafts of the Ecton Copper Mines.

THOR'S CAVE & ECTON HILL

DISTANCE: 13.6KM/8.5MILES » **TOTAL ASCENT:** 370M/1,220FT » **START GR:** SK 102593 » **TIME:** ALLOW 5 HOURS **MAP:** OS EXPLORER OL24 WHITE PEAK, 1:25000 » **REFRESHMENTS:** ROYAL OAK AT WETTON. NATIONAL TRUST TEASHOP AT WETTONMILL » **NAVIGATION:** DEMANDS CONCENTRATION ON THE ASCENT OF ECTON HILL

Directions – Thor's Cave &
Ecton Hill

➊ Follow the Manifold Way as far as the road tunnel. **Turn left**, follow the road across the river, then **turn right**. Follow the lane/track to Wettonmill.

2 Cross the bridge, then the road, and cross the footbridge by a ford to gain the old road down the valley (quieter than the road that follows the old track bed). Where the roads meet, **bear right** along the Manifold Way and continue for a further 700m to a footbridge across the river (often dry in summer).

3 Cross it and follow the paved path up to Thor's Cave. Continue up immediately left of the cave along a path that leads to a track. **Turn left** and continue to a road.

4 **Bear right**, then **fork left** into Wetton village and continue to the first right-hand bend (or **fork right** for public toilets and the Royal Oak, then **keep left** to reach the aforementioned bend).

5 **Turn left** (or go **straight on** if approaching from the pub) and **fork left** immediately along a track, then keep **straight on** along a footpath. Pass over a col then descend with a wall on the left. Cross either of two footbridges, then continue uphill along a track/road to a fork in about 500m.

6 **Fork left**, then in 100m **turn right** through a gate. Keep **straight on** uphill along a path, passing old spoil heaps, then other mining relics. The main path passes right of the summit but others lead up left to the triangulation pillar. Continue down the ridge to a former engine house, passing close to several deep shafts.

7 Cross a stile **straight ahead**, then **turn sharp right** to follow the track down to a road. **Turn left** and follow the road down to a T-junction. **Turn right** into Westside Mill.

8 **Turn left** as signposted to cross the river by a footbridge, then **bear left** to join the Manifold Way. (Often wet to the right). **Turn right** to finish.

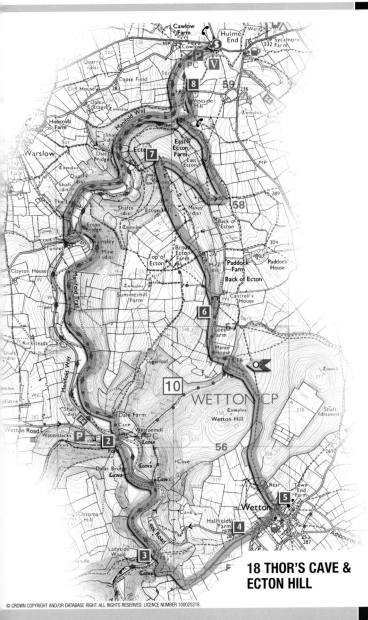

18 THOR'S CAVE & ECTON HILL

MONSAL DALE PHOTO: JOHN COEFIELD

19 Longstone Moor & Cressbrook Dale 15.8km/9.8miles

This route combines a climb to a moorland hilltop, a visit to a quaint old village, and a walk through a limestone gorge.

Monsal Head » Little Longstone » Longstone Moor » Foolow » Wardlow Mires » Cressbrook Dale » Cressbrook » Monsal Head

Start

Monsal Head pay and display car park, just over 1.5km northwest of Ashford-in-the-Water on the B6465. GR: SK 185715.

The Walk

Monsal Head, where our walk starts, is one of the Peak District's most accessible viewpoints. It overlooks the dramatic deep valley of the River Wye as it flows through Monsal Dale and beneath the arches of the former railway viaduct that spans the gorge.

From here, our route climbs through fields and along old tracks to the cairn at the top of Longstone Moor. This is also the site of an ancient tumulus, or burial mound – a commanding location, from which there are distant views of the moors, the gritstone edges and the limestone uplands. Moving on, we gradually descend off the moor and through fields to take us to the village of Foolow, with its quaint cottages, its 14th Century market cross and village pond.

Paths that cross wildflower meadows lead us downhill to Cressbrook Dale. The Three Stags Head, opposite the head of the dale, is always worth a visit. Entering is like stepping back in time, as the interior of the pub echoes its outward appearance.

The path leads straight into the dale and soon passes the prominent limestone rock known as Peter's Stone, then climbs the valley side only to descend again. The climb is worth it, however, since the view back up the dale is quite stunning, while in May and June, a fine display of wild flowers makes for a rewarding descent.

Our route continues through woodland and down into Cressbrook to enter Water-cum-Jolly. The river here forms a mill pond before tumbling over an impressive weir. The last leg takes the Monsal Trail and crosses the viaduct, then makes the short climb back to Monsal Head to finish.

LONGSTONE MOOR & CRESSBROOK DALE

DISTANCE: 15.8KM/9.8MILES » **TOTAL ASCENT:** 465M/1,520FT » **START GR:** SK 185715 » **TIME:** ALLOW 5 HOURS **MAP:** OS EXPLORER OL24 WHITE PEAK, 1:25000 » **REFRESHMENTS:** BULL'S HEAD AT FOOLOW. THREE STAG'S HEAD AT WARDLOW MIRES, WEEKENDS ONLY » **NAVIGATION:** ALL ON ESTABLISHED FOOTPATHS BUT DEMANDS CONCENTRATION ON LONGSTONE MOOR.

Directions – Longstone Moor & Cressbrook Dale

➏ Cross the main road and follow the pavement to Little Longstone. Take the path **left** by the side of the Packhorse Inn, signposted *Chertpit Lane*. Pass through a handgate, then 50m on the right, another. Continue with the wall on the left and through a third handgate. **Bear slightly right** towards a solitary tree and fingerpost beyond it. Cross a stile and continue uphill on the more obvious path.

2 On emerging at a track, **turn right** and follow this for 500m, then **turn left** into an enclosure with picnic area sign. Cross a stile on the **left** and continue uphill to a wall with stile.

DIRECTIONS CONTINUE OVERLEAF

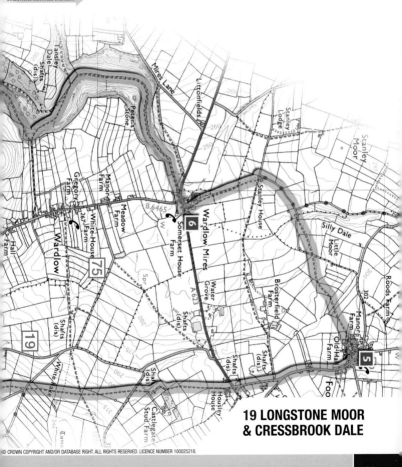

19 LONGSTONE MOOR & CRESSBROOK DALE

3 Cross this and **turn right**. Walk uphill parallel with the wall to join an obvious path, then **turn right** and continue up to the cairn. Continue between two copses. The path reaches a path crossroads in 500m at the end of the first of two enclosures on the right.

4 **Turn left**, head for a solitary hawthorn, then **fork left** up to a fingerpost. Continue downhill, cross a stile, then **bear slightly right**. Maintain this direction across fields, crossing a road, a track, another road, then a farm access road. Follow a high wall enclosing a wood round to a stile between gates. Continue across more fields to houses and the main road at Housley. Follow the road opposite into Foolow.

5 **Turn left** at the junction. Walk to the **left** of the pond and keep **straight ahead** to a half-hidden fingerpost, then follow the alleyway to a gate. **Bear half right** to a hand-gate, then follow the obvious path through fields. Cross an old walled track and continue in the same direction to join the track further on. **Bear right** and continue to a track junction, then **bear left** to a farmhouse. Leave the track at the bend to cross the stile on the left, then take the **right fork** downhill. Keep a wall on the right, then pass between farm buildings to reach the main road at Wardlow Mires.

6 **Turn right**, cross the main road then the Wardlow Road and **bear left** to pass in front of Brookside Farm. Go through a gate and enter Cressbrook Dale. Walk down the dale, pass beneath Peter's Stone, then **bear left** up the hillside. (A path runs along the valley bottom through woods but misses the stunning views.) At the top of the valley side **bear right** before a wall to follow the path in descent. The path requires care over a rock step. Continue across a footbridge and stay on the bottom footpath. Pass cottages at Ravensdale, follow the lane up to a junction, then descend to a junction at Cressbrook.

7 Take the path to the **right**, passing in front of Cressbrook Mill Apartments. Where the path meets the pool, **turn left**, cross the footbridge over the torrent below the weir and continue up to the Monsal Trail. Follow this south to where it runs through a tunnel immediately after crossing the viaduct, then follow the path up to Monsal Head.

CRESSBROOK DALE PHOTO: JON BARTON **115**

LOWER DOVE DALE BELOW THORPE CLOUD PHOTO: JOHN COEFIELD

20 Dove Dale & Bunster Hill

13.5km/8.5miles

This walk includes a limestone gorge with spectacular rock features and crags, a particularly attractive upland village, and a hilltop with superb views.

Dove Dale » Milldale » Alstonefield » Stanshope » Hall Dale » Ilam Tops » Bunster Hill » Dove Dale

Start

Dove Dale car park, situated equidistant from Thorpe and Ilam, northwest of Ashbourne and 4km west of the A515. GR: SK 147509.

The Walk

Our walk starts by following a path upstream into the narrow limestone gorge of Dove Dale. The path passes beneath the steep flanks of Thorpe Cloud, a former reef knoll that grew from the sea bed in a limey tropical sea over 300 million years ago. Further on we come to the impressive Tissington Spires, the natural arch near Reynard's Cave and Lion's Head Rock. On the other side of the Dove is the tower-like Ilam Rock.

Six hundred metres further upstream, we come to Dove Holes, which were etched out by the river when it flowed as a torrent at a higher level. Eventually, the path crosses an ancient packhorse bridge and enters the hamlet of Milldale.

Our route leaves the gorge at this point to climb to Alstonefield. This is a delightful upland village of old stone cottages, an Elizabethan Manor House and a 15th Century church. The route loses height from Alstonefield, only to climb again, giving us the chance to descend one of Dove Dale's tributary dales.

Hall Dale is a dry valley, down which the path drops steeply over a few metres near the confluence. Alas, our route climbs again from here, this time up steps – lots of them – leading up to the top of a steep wooded slope. A narrow path, which requires care, continues across the top of the woods.

Suddenly, the path emerges into the open at Ilam Tops to reveal a breathtaking view across the gorge. It crosses high pastures to reach the top of Bunster Hill overlooking Ilam. After a grassy descent a path leads us across the flanks of the hill back to the start.

DOVE DALE & BUNSTER HILL

DISTANCE: 13.5KM/8.5MILES » **TOTAL ASCENT:** 560M/1,830FT » **START GR:** SK 147509 » **TIME:** ALLOW 5 HOURS **MAP:** OS EXPLORER OL24 WHITE PEAK, 1:25000 » **REFRESHMENTS:** IZAAK WALTON HOTEL NEAR THE START AND FINISH OR SMALL SHOP AT THE CAR PARK. TEAS AND REFRESHMENTS BUT NO CAFÉ AT MILLDALE, THE GEORGE AND TEASHOP AT ALSTONEFIELD » **NAVIGATION:** STRAIGHTFORWARD, ALTHOUGH THERE IS A NEED FOR CONCENTRATION AT ILAM TOPS ABOVE DOVE DALE.

Directions – Dove Dale & Bunster Hill

⮕ From the car park walk past the toilet block, follow the track upstream on the left of the river then cross over using the stepping stones. If the river is high cross the footbridge and continue on the right bank. The path improves in 300m. If the river is low, stay on the left side, then cross at stepping stones. Continue up the gorge on the undulating path for 4km, where the path crosses the river by an old packhorse bridge to enter Milldale.

2 **Turn left**, then **first right** and pass in front of Polly's Cottage to follow Millway Lane uphill to Alstonefield. 150m beyond the church **bear left**, then keep **straight on** to a junction.

3 **Turn left**, then take the first track on the **left** (50m). Keep **straight on** along this to where it bends sharp right. Leave the track, cross the stile and keep **straight on** with a wall on the right. Cross a stile and **bear right** with the wall to descend steeply to a road. Cross the road and continue up the track opposite. This leads to the hamlet of Stanshope.

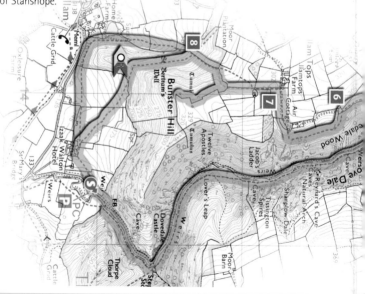

4 At the junction, **turn left** along a track then in 100m cross the stile on the **right**. Follow the path across fields, down into Hall Dale and so to the River Dove.

5 **Turn right** and walk downstream alongside the river to a waymark post in 150m. **Bear right** to follow the stepped footpath up to the top of the woods and the valley side. Continue along the top edge of the wood along a narrow footpath. Eventually the path exits the wood at a stile.

DIRECTIONS CONTINUE OVERLEAF ▶

20 DOVE DALE & BUNSTER HILL

Directions – Dove Dale & Bunster Hill

6 **Bear slightly left** downhill as directed by the fingerpost. The path becomes narrow as it skirts below an isolated cottage then **bears right** through two stiles on its far side to emerge on the cottage drive. **Turn left** and follow this as far as the gateway to Ilamtops Farm.

7 **Turn left** and walk along the avenue of trees and through a gate. Keep **straight on** here with a wall on the right. Cross a stile in the corner ahead (Bunster Hill sign). Keep more or less **straight on** to the top of Bunster Hill. Retrace your steps as far as the stile. Instead of crossing it **turn left** and descend with a wall on the right. Ignore a stile on the right in 100m and continue as far as a definite path cross roads with a stile on the right.

8 **Turn left** here to follow the badly eroded and awkward path across the steep flanks of Bunster Hill. Continue through a gap on the ridge, then **bear left** downhill. Cross a stile and maintain the same direction across fields to the back of the Izaak Walton Hotel, then **bear left** to return to the car park.

> ⬤OR A safer and easier, but often muddy, alternative is to continue downhill and skirt Bunster Hill by joining the footpath that leads from Ilam to Dove Dale car park.

DOVE DALE *PHOTO: JOHN COEFIELD* **121**

Written by local authors, each book features:

» 20 great day-length circular walks
» Invaluable local area information
» Ordnance Survey maps
» Easy-to-use directions

Day Walks in the
North York **Moors**
20 circular routes in
North Yorkshire

Written by
Tony Harker

Day Walks in
Snowdonia
20 circular routes in
North Wales

Written by
Tom Hutton

Appendix

The following is a list of Tourist Information Centres, shops, cafes, pubs, websites and other contacts that might come in handy.

Tourist Information Centres

www.visitpeakdistrict.com – Official tourism website for the Peak District & Derbyshire.
www.peakdistrict.org – Official website of the Peak District National Park Authority.

Ashbourne	T: 01335 343 666
Bakewell	T: 01629 816 558
Buxton	T: 01298 25 106
Castleton	T: 01629 816 558
Edale	T: 01433 670 207
Fairholmes,	
Upper Derwent Valley	T: 01433 650 953
Glossop	T: 01457 869 176
Manifold Valley (Hartington)	T: 01298 84 679
Matlock	T: 01629 583 388

Food and Drink
Cafes
(See individual routes for recommendations.)
Café On The Green, Baslow T: 01246 583 000
Three Roofs Café, Castleton T: 01433 620 533
Stables Teashop, Chatsworth and Garden Centre Café at Calton Lees.
Pool Café, Hathersage T: 01433 651 159 also Cintra's Tea Room, T: 01433 651 825
Hassop Station Café, Hassop, T: 01629 815 668
Ilam Park Tea Room in the grounds of Ilam Hall, Ilam.
Langnor Craft Centre & Coffee Shop, Longnor T: 01298 835 87 also Cobbles Tea &

Coffee Shop, T: 01298 831 66
The School Rooms, Low Bradfield
T: 01142 851 920
Old Smithy, Monyash, T: 01629 810 190
Country Parlour Café at
Caudwell's Mill, Rowsley T: 01629 733 185
Vanilla Kitchen tea room, Tideswell
T: 01298 871 519
The Old Coach House, Tissington
T: 01335 350 501
Roaches Tea Rooms, Upper Hulme
T: 01538 300 345

Pubs
(See individual routes for recommendations.)

Barrel Inn, Bretton	T: 01433 630 856
Bull's Head, Foolow	T: 01433 630 873
Grouse Inn, Froggatt	T: 01433 630 423
Bull's Head, Monyash	T: 01629 812 372
Ye Olde Royal Oak, Wetton	T: 01335 310 287
Cat and Fiddle	T: 01298 23 364
Cheshire Cheese, Hope	T: 01433 620 330
The Druid Inn, Birchover	T: 01629 650 302
The Fox House Inn	T: 01433 631 708
Ladybower Inn	T: 01433 651 241
The Monsal Head Hotel	T: 01629 640 250
The Red Lion, Litton	T: 01298 871 458
The Royal Hotel, Hayfield	T: 01633 742 721

Accommodation
Youth Hostels
YHA Youth Hostels can be found in the following places. For more information please visit www.yha.org.uk

Castleton	T: 0845 371 9628
Crowden	T: 0845 371 9113

Edale   T: 0845 371 9514
Hartington   T: 0845 371 9740
Hathersage   T: 0845 371 9021
Ravenstor   T: 0845 371 9655
Youlgreave   T: 0845 371 9151

Bunkhouses, B&Bs and Hotels
www.peakdistrictonline.co.uk
For specific information, contact a Tourist
Information Centre in the area in which you
intend to stay.

Camping
(There are many more in the Peak District; search
online or call a local Tourist Information Centre.)
North Lees, Hathersage   T: 01433 650 838
Eric Byne, Baslow   T: 01246 582 277

Weather
www.meto.gov.uk   www.metcheck.com

Outdoor Shops
CCC Outdoors – Hathersage
www.gooutdoors.co.uk   T: 01433 659 870

Outside – Calver
www.outside.co.uk   T: 01433 631 111

Outside – Hathersage
www.outside.co.uk   T: 01433 651 936

Jo Royle Outdoor – Buxton
www.jo-royle.co.uk   T: 01298 25 824

The Square – Hathersage
www.thesquareshop.co.uk   T: 01433 698 109

Cotswold Outdoor – Bakewell
www.cotswoldoutdoor.com   T: 01629 812 231

Hitch n Hike – Bamford
www.hitchnhike.co.uk   T: 01433 651 013

Other Publications
Day Walks In The Peak District:
20 New Circular Routes
Norman Taylor and Barry Pope, Vertebrate
Publishing – www.v-publishing.co.uk

Peak Summits: Eight Classic Walks (Laminated Map)
Jon Barton, Vertebrate Publishing –
www.v-publishing.co.uk

Peak District Climbing
John Coefield & Jon Barton, Vertebrate Publishing –
www.v-publishing.co.uk

Peak District Bouldering
Rupert Davies, John Coefield, Jon Barton,
Vertebrate Publishing – www.v-publishing.co.uk

Cycling in the Peak District:
Off-Road Trails & Quiet Lanes
Tom Fenton & Jon Barton, Vertebrate Publishing –
www.v-publishing.co.uk

Peak District Mountain Biking – Dark Peak Trails
Jon Barton, Vertebrate Publishing –
www.v-publishing.co.uk

White Peak Mountain Biking – The Pure Trails
Jon Barton, Vertebrate Publishing –
www.v-publishing.co.uk

About the Authors

Norman Taylor has been a climber and fell walker since his teens. Since becoming a father with two children in the 1980s he began to plan walks to suit a young family. This resulted in his first publication, Family Walks in the White Peak. This spawned a nationwide series for Scarthin Books of Cromford, and Norman himself wrote a further five Family Walks guides. Since leaving the teaching profession and becoming manager of Foothills – the Outdoor Specialists in Sheffield – some years ago, he has been leading weekly, guided walks throughout the Peak District. The two Peak District *Day Walks* guidebooks, published by Vertebrate Publishing, are his latest project based on an intimate knowledge of the National Park.

To help him in the venture, Norman enlisted friend and walking companion **Barry Pope**. A keen fell walker since his teens, Barry for many years roamed, explored and photographed the landscape of the Peak District National Park. In the process, he acquired an enviable knowledge of the natural history and archaeology of the area.

Vertebrate Publishing

Vertebrate Publishing an independent publisher dedicated to producing the very best outdoor leisure titles. We have critically acclaimed and award-winning titles covering a range of leisure activities, including; mountain biking, cycling, rock climbing, hill walking and others. We are best known for our own titles such as *Lake District Mountain Biking*, and *Revelations* – the autobiography of British rock climber Jerry Moffatt, awarded the **Grand Prize** at the **2009 Banff Mountain Book Festival**. For more information about Vertebrate Publishing please visit our website: **www.v-publishing.co.uk**